Photography Editor: RICHARD MAACK
Book Designer: MARY WINKELMAN VELGOS
Copy Editors: EVELYN HOWELL and PK PERKIN McMAHON
Book Editor: BOB ALBANO
Map: KEVIN KIBSEY

Library of Congress Control Number: 2005924338
ISBN-10: 1-893860-99-X
ISBN-13: 978-1-893860-99-5
First printing, 2005. Second printing, 2006. Third printing, 2008.
Fourth printing, 2008. Fifth printing, 2009. Printed in Singapore.

Published by the Book Division of *Arizona Highways*® magazine, a monthly
publication of the Arizona Department of Transportation, 2039 West Lewis Avenue,
Phoenix, Arizona 85009.
Telephone: (602) 712-2200
Web site: www.arizonahighways.com

Publisher: WIN HOLDEN
Editor: ROBERT STIEVE
Senior Editor/Books: RANDY SUMMERLIN
Director of Photography: PETER ENSENBERGER
Production Director: MICHAEL BIANCHI
Production Coordinator: ANNETTE PHARES

Secret Sedona

Sacred Moments in the Landscape

TEXT AND PHOTOGRAPHS BY LARRY LINDAHL

Left, viewed from Schnebly Hill, a sunset casts fiery colors on monsoon clouds over 6,355-foot Capitol Butte (left) and an adjacent 5,977-foot promontory the author nicknamed "Pinnacle Peak."

Page 1, Cathedral Rock.

Above, a dragon fly rests.

Foreword

Adventure

IS IT SERENDIPITY or fate that we cross paths with another? Among millions of human lives, we touch only a few. I met Larry Lindahl by sheer chance while on a twilight walk near the end of a road in Yarnell, Arizona. I've ceased to question the deeper, underlying matrix of connections that bring people together. On that first meeting we conversed about life's meaning and the magical desert surrounding us, and we discovered a common interest in art, literature, and music. I was in Yarnell, with Christine, my wife and partner, doing a two-week program at the local elementary school through the Arizona Commission on the Arts.

During those two weeks, a friendship began. An invitation for Larry to create the album cover for one of my musical collaborations with Native American flutist R. Carlos Nakai led to a professional relationship as well. Larry's talents as a photographer, artist, and graphic designer became integral to creating a new design style, over the next 12 years, for Canyon Records, the Native American record label in Phoenix.

Since meeting Larry, I have admired the way in which he views the world. Through the practice of his art and the lens of a camera, he has studied in great detail the gathering of light and the presence of form. Somehow all of these intense moments of concentration have imbued his vocabulary with a rich sonority of texture and tone. In this book, he takes us to places where we've never been before. We are there, with him, in the stillness and the movement that flows with the tempo of the wild — the rush of the wind, the rhythm of the waters, the echo of a canyon. His journal brings sublime imagery and subtle nuance into vivid focus.

Scientists tell us that the perceptual experience of our memory and seeing the actual thing are the same in our mind. Our ancestors in their oral tradition employed storytelling as a mnemonic device to recount important events. Larry's journal, like the ancient stories, allows the surrounding landscape to speak to us and tell us its tale. We enter a canyon and then a dwelling built with the earth and are

reminded of a different time when we knew each plant, each tree, each birdcall, and the clouds and breeze spoke to us. This was not so long ago. And the memories still reside deep within our human physiology.

As you begin reading this journal, remind yourself of the tens of thousands of years of human evolution when survival required that our senses be tuned to the rhythms of a complex, diverse natural world. Remember a mind capable of engaging its full attention on this present moment and a living, participatory landscape.

Perhaps, before you continue, quiet your mind and recall walks you've taken in the landscape. Enjoy the adventure that is about to unfold, where this magical desert allows us a brief glimpse into eternity.

— William Eaton

Musician William Eaton (above) has composed for and performed with numerous groups and orchestras, including his own William Eaton Ensemble. His recordings include two collaborations with R. Carlos Nakai that received Grammy nominations. He designs and builds unique stringed instruments, which have received broad acclaim. Eaton and his family live in Sedona.

At left, ancient-sounding melodies reverberate from a primitive bow-stringed instrument played by William Eaton. He performs with a unique collection of stringed instruments that he designs and builds, including a harp guitar, above.

Sacred Moments

People say that what we're all seeking is a meaning for life. I think that what we're seeking is an experience of being alive, so that our life experiences . . . will have resonance within our own innermost being and reality, so that we actually feel the rapture of being alive.

— Joseph Campbell, *The Power of Myth*

EARLY ONE FEBRUARY morning, I walked into a fog-shrouded Boynton Canyon. Misty winter rain soaked the sandstone dark red. Waterfalls, flowing for only a short while, broadcast their sounds into the air. The clouds began dissolving in late-morning, and the sandstone cliffs reflected a deep, wet purple under the opening sky.

By afternoon I had hiked to a large alcove and was sitting spellbound, watching a transparent curtain of water cascading over the opening. I could see the canyon through the falling water as it glistened and wavered with sparks of light. An ancient Indian ruin stood behind me. I wondered about people of the past. Had the Ancient Ones watched this same scene transfixed, as I was, by its magic?

The moment felt timeless, without boundaries. The past and present and future seemed as one reality, holistic, yet ephemeral. I sensed the cycle of water, falling from clouds into streams flowing to the ocean, only to return again as clouds. I sensed the ancient existence of humans and animals and plants and the Earth.

Everything seemed richly integrated. I felt baptized into some kind of knowing — like the sacred essence of life had just been revealed, to me, for the first time. It was a moment I will never forget.

The next morning I began writing about the experience. At first, my handwriting filled one page, and then another. When I finally set down the pen, words covered eight full-sized pages. I soon bought a 6x9-inch notebook, my first field journal. I took it with me everywhere — trips to Monument Valley, down the Colorado River, and on my journeys through the red rocks of Sedona. Keeping the journal became a way to bring home the story of my experiences, to preserve the sensations, scents, and sounds a camera cannot record. The book you are holding was born in that notebook.

Season after season, I went out into the red rock landscape. Year after year, I found bleached bones, antlers, animal skulls, feathers, and stones. I left behind ancient grinding stones, a multitude of decorated potsherds, a bone awl, digging sticks, and a palette smeared with ancient pictograph paint. I left these artifacts where I found them. I knew they belonged to the land. They are part of its story.

Capturing the best light of the day often meant hiking back in twilight or in the dark. In the dim lighting, I accidentally startled deer, javelina, lizards, quail, and rattlesnakes. My cheek was brushed once with the wing of a low-flying bat (it felt soft like peach fuzz). I startled myself several times with "rattlesnakes" that were actually just exposed tree roots.

Carrying a backpack and spending the night in my sleeping bag offered new possibilities to make unique photos. From the summit of Capitol Butte, I once photographed the rising full moon in January. Light from the west tinted Soldiers Pass and Wilson Mountain in

sunset colors as the moon broke over the eastern horizon. To the north, the snow-covered San Francisco Peaks turned pink. As the sun disappeared, the temperature plunged. I made my way down the mountain the following morning.

Working on a photography assignment for *Arizona Highways*, I stayed several days on Secret Mountain, alone. One summer night, after a nearly cloudless sunset, a thunderstorm arrived around midnight. Crackling lightning speared the mountaintop. The air smelled acrid with ozone. I prayed for sunrise. The next morning — under a calm, overcast sky — I awoke exhausted, but thankful to be alive.

I tried solo backpacking down the 12-mile length of West Fork Canyon in late autumn. Sleeping the first night on a sandbar I was nearly stepped on in the dark by a running deer or elk. Worse by far, was early — very early — the next morning when the "slight chance of rain" forecast became 100 percent. To save on weight I hadn't brought a tent, only a tarp. It couldn't keep me dry, and rain drenched my down sleeping bag. The bugle call of

"retreat" sounded in my head. I turned around and went home.

Injuries and discomfort, yes there were a few. But, effort, discomfort, and sometimes pain heighten the exhilaration of finding a hidden waterfall, or a ruin, or the view from a mountain summit. I unknowingly encountered poison ivy on several hikes (keep your eye out for it in West Fork). I experienced the most intense pain while hiking cross-country about 3 miles from my van. A large rock up in the Margs Draw area had rolled onto the back of my leg. I went to Sedona Urgent Care for an x-ray. The doctor confirmed that the leg was severely bruised, but not broken. Serge Wright, my eye doctor, also patched me back together after a sharp branch scraped my eyeball as I was bushwhacking out of a side canyon.

As you turn to the following pages, keep in mind Albert Einstein's observation that "the most beautiful thing we can experience is the mysterious. It is the source of all art and science."

Now, enter the mystery and beauty of Sedona. Share moments captured by camera

and field journal and years of exploring. You may soon sense the spirit of the Earth reawakening your soul. Here, in this land of deer tracks and desert plants, bird flight and wild flowers, you will take your own inner landscape — the wild and sacred space within yourself. Forgotten dreams may drift back into view. Creative desires begin to howl, seeking a place in your busy schedule. Adventurous ideas might begin to transform, from impractical to truly possible. Feel your spirit energize among the luminous sandstone formations, refreshing forest scent, and sound of tumbling creek water.

You may take the time to relax and rest for awhile at a special place. Without the distractions of your motion or spoken words you will begin to hear the mysterious and inspiring silence. At first you may hear nothing, and then you may begin to hear everything.

"Be alert," says Barry Lopez in *Arctic Dreams*, "for that moment when something sacred reveals itself within the mundane and you know the land knows you are there." You will understand. ○

Above, the setting sun casts an ethereal glow over (left to right) Gibraltar, Cathedral Rock, the Nuns, and Twin Buttes, all seen from a vantage point on Munds Mountain.

Left, a butterfly flits over a bouquet of fleabane.

Chapter 1

Into the Mystery

The mystery of life is not a problem to be solved but a reality to be experienced.

— Aart van der Leeuw, *The Soul Unearthed*

OUT FROM UNDER THE FIERCE June sun, Kathleen and I catch our breath in a cave high above a side canyon. A quiet breeze sends a dry, desert scent dancing along the cool, shaded stone, giving a whisper of comfort. We are deep in the Red Rock-Secret Mountain Wilderness, northwest of Sedona.

On the trek here, we worked through slopes of thorny catclaw that tore at our bare legs. Dizzy from the heat, I only half-consciously felt each sharp, new pain. To gain the next higher level in the canyon, we pulled ourselves up through an eroded space barely as wide as my shoulders. Breaking out again into the sunlight, we followed a ledge over a series of cliffs to the top of a talus slope. Tall prickly pear taunted us until only 20 feet separated us from our goal — 20 vertical feet.

Our eyes searched this last obstacle hoping the ancient Indians had chiseled handholds and footholds into the cliff. They hadn't, so with fingertips clinging to thin cracks, we slowly pulled ourselves up and — at last — inside the cave.

The view now sweeps over the valley below, over ridges and rock formations, until the openness is walled in by the massive architecture of abruptly rising, beautifully weathered sandstone cliffs. Narrow shelves, ledges, and inaccessible terraces support stunted piñon and juniper trees. Cactus drapes over stone edges. Clumps of bear grass, agave, and strawberry hedgehog live undisturbed beneath even taller cliffs. Standing in the cave is an ancient Indian dwelling, multi-roomed and in nearly perfect condition.

We first caught a glimpse of the ruin at the beginning of the year when we paused on a day hike to drink hot chocolate. We took turns looking around with compact binoculars. The dull sky discretely brightened as I took my turn. Pale, winter light angled low into an opening in the distant cliff face. In that moment this well-hidden ruin was revealed to us.

In the preceding panel [pages 10 and 11], the sunset's glow reddens Capitol Butte and the rock formations of Mitten Ridge.

Nestled among Arizona cypress trees, left, a round shelter hides in an alcove above the Dry Creek Basin northwest of Sedona. Prehistoric Sinagua Indians built such structures throughout the area's red rock canyons. One of them, Red Canyon, above, displays pictographs and petroglyphs on the cliff walls.

Now, inside the cave, I look at high stone walls built centuries ago. Constructed of large stones covered with smooth, mud plaster, the walls divide rooms and dim chambers deeper in the cave. I envision the work it must have taken to build this place.

The builders first would have gathered dozens upon dozens of heavy, square-sided stones. Dirt — plenty of it — and water had to be collected to be mixed into mortar and plaster. Several trees with reasonably straight trunks were cut for beams, headers, and door lintels. Imagine cutting down a tree with a stone ax!

Workers lifted all the wood, stones, dirt, and water to the cave. They marked room outlines, placed the largest stones, packed mud mortar between each stone, and pressed bits of sandstone into the mortar to minimize the shrinkage as it dried. They trimmed wood for door lintels, fitting the ends into the walls, and added stone and mud above them.

After constructing each room, workers mixed finishing plaster and spread it over each wall with the palms of their hands. Small fingerprints in the plaster show that the kids were helping, too. Then, layer upon layer, workers coated the packed-earth floor with mud plaster. When the final coat dried, the floor was hard, durable, and easy to sweep clean. After many weeks, or maybe several months, the entire family must have shared in the feeling of completion after finishing such a tremendous accomplishment. Muscle-aching work, all of it.

Today, the east end of the front wall now slumps with age, pinching the doorway. Carefully, Kathleen and I turn sideways and slip through the opening. Steps lead to more rooms with walls smoke-stained by many fires. I imagine the family, long ago, around a flickering fire huddled against the dark of winter.

HOPI INDIANS ARE the modern-day descendants of these ancient people. Their ancestors passed down stories for each succeeding generation to learn and pass on. Stories told of people emerging from underworlds into this, the Fourth World, and of migrations

where the people simply left their homes and moved on in the continued search for their foretold Center of the World.

Thus, the family, or clan, abandoned this cliff house. Carrying only a few household items, along with memories, they simply walked away. Their migrations finally led them from the land of red rocks to their Center Place that we know today as the First, Second, and Third mesas of the Hopi.

In the early part of the 20th century, the name *Sinagua* (sin-AH-wah) was chosen for the Indian culture that built the ancient stone dwellings we find in Verde Valley, Sedona, and up around Flagstaff. The term comes from *Sierra sin Agua* (Mountain without Water), the name Spanish explorers gave to the tall, snow-covered mountain just north of the red rocks. (Later, Franciscan missionaries renamed it the San Francisco Peaks.)

Before the Sinagua — 6,000 to possibly 10,000 years ago — small bands of post-Ice Age hunters and gatherers roamed vast territories in the Southwest, including the lands of present-day Sedona. Spear tips made of stone, called Clovis points, are among the few artifacts archaeologists have to study from that period. In a canyon northwest of Sedona, a man working on his land unearthed a nearly perfect Clovis point in February 2003. The discovery lit up the archaeological community. Only a handful

of Clovis points — all broken — had been discovered in central and northern Arizona.

The hunters devised a specialized throwing system to throw the Clovis point at targets. The three-piece weapon, called an atlatl, had a spear shaft, a detachable fore shaft including the Clovis point, and a wooden throwing handle about the length of one's forearm. The handle significantly boosted throwing power to penetrate the thick skin of large mammals.

Other remnants of the pre-Sinagua people have emerged. Several years ago, ancient split-twig figurines were discovered near Sedona in a dry cave in Sycamore Canyon, a tributary of the Verde River. Pliable willow saplings had been split partway down, then carefully bent and wrapped into animal shapes — perhaps deer, elk, or bighorn sheep. The palm-sized figurines are nearly identical to ones discovered at Stanton's Cave and Cremation Canyon in the Grand Canyon. Thorns or other objects found piercing the animal's side suggest these 3,000- to 4,000-year-old animal fetishes were used in hunting or ritual magic.

Based on traces of agriculture and pieces of broken pottery, archaeologists believe the Sinagua

Sinagua Indians built this dwelling, above, deep into a cliff face in the Red Rock-Secret Mountain Wilderness. Two front rooms overlook a side canyon, while stone stairs lead to more enclosures deeper in the cave.

At right, sunset brightens a crumbling, centuries-old structure precariously isolated high above Lost Canyon.

Clockwise from above left are a Sinagua ruin in a cave and the ruins of Honanki and Lomaki. The ruin in the cave, located in Boynton Canyon, is one of the sites involved in a Yavapai creation story. West of Sedona, Honanki housed an active Sinagua population in more than 60 rooms from A.D. 1130 to 1280. More recently, Yavapai Indians painted the glyphs above the stone buildings long after the Sinagua population had moved on. Lomaki, meaning "Beautiful House" in Hopi, sits with the snow-covered San Francisco Peaks in view at Wupatki National Monument.

began to appear in the Verde Valley and east of the San Francisco Peaks around A.D. 650-700. Coconino National Forest archaeologist Peter Pilles claims that one of the most significant characteristics of the Sinagua was a "willingness to accept and experiment with new customs" learned through "relationships with other cultures."

By A.D. 1000, trade systems involving other cultures crisscrossed Sinagua territory.

To the north and northeast, around the Four Corners area, the Kayenta Ancestral Puebloan Culture thrived. Its people reigned as experts of decorated pottery and masonry construction — think of Mesa Verde and Chaco Canyon. (In

recent years, the term Ancestral Puebloans has been adopted to refer to what once was called the Anasazi culture.) Winslow Puebloan Culture occupied the Little Colorado River basin to the east. To the southeast, people of the Mogollon Culture, perhaps inspired by neighboring cultures, were making Salado redware and beautiful, yet haunting, Mimbres pottery. The Hohokam Culture, to the south in what now is Phoenix, developed advanced irrigation systems and trade connections reaching deep into Mayan-era Mexico. Just over the mountains west of Sedona lived people of the Prescott Culture, who, it's been suggested, brewed a fermented drink. And to the northwest was the Cohonina Culture, whose name is reflected in

Ancient Sinagua Indians painstakingly collected water from places like this source near Fay Canyon. Then, with heavy ceramic jugs strapped to their backs, they returned across treacherous ledges to their cliff houses.

the names for Coconino sandstone and Coconino National Forest.

Sinaguan cotton textiles, woven with intricate geometric patterns, and salt gathered from near present-day Camp Verde were valued trade items in exchange for decorated ceramic wares, copper bells, turquoise, and colorful macaw feathers. The Sinagua also carved argillite, or pipestone, from near Prescott into ornaments and beads, and they fashioned seashells from the Sea of Cortes and the Pacific Coast into bracelets and pendants.

As boys grew up destined to be farmers, elders taught them the secrets of the land. How cold air, similar to water, flows downhill. How it moves at night off mesa tops, sinks down through canyons, and collects in low-lying places, therefore making the longest growing season atop mesas, not in the river valleys. The older men would have told the boys that their corn needed 130 frost-free days to mature into edible food. Boys also learned that summer rains fell more in the uplands than in the valleys. Always look for places to plant, their fathers would have said. Be cautious, for the first places to lose the

winter cold will also be the first places to lose moisture to the summer sun. Fathers would have encouraged their sons to plant crops in a variety of places to ensure the family would have enough food.

Likewise, mothers shared their knowledge with their daughters. Know the ways of the wild plants, they would have told the young girls. As wild foods ripened, the women collected nuts, seeds, beans, fruit, and herbs. Nearly every day the women took handfuls of dried corn from the storage jars and ground it with stones into flour. Wise, older women would have shared knowledge of where buckwheat, amaranth, and rice grass could be found and how to collect and prepare the protein-rich seeds. Grandmothers may have told about piñon trees and the three-year cycle of pine nut harvest. Older girls learned when to dig the agave root and about the four-day roasting process to make the heart-meat found inside taste sweet. Girls learned about reliable springs, places to look for watercress and wild mint.

So many lessons to learn as one generation passed knowledge to the next. Their lives depended on it.

JUST AFTER THE growing season of A.D. 1064, the Earth violently erupted just east of the San Francisco Peaks, less than 40 miles from present-day Sedona. Bright-red lava spurted from a fissure nearly 10 miles long in a dramatic curtain of fire. Oozing lava flowed 5 miles eastward. Hot cinders spewed into the sky and rained onto the land and pit houses for 2 miles around the volcano. After 50 years, and many eruptions, cinders from Sunset Crater had fallen over some 800 square miles, including areas as far east as Kansas.

Many pit houses were destroyed, but no bodies have been found in them, suggesting the people had time to evacuate.

Lucky for the southern Sinagua living below the Mogollon Rim that the prevailing winds protected their homeland. But

the dramatic eruption became legend to everyone living in the region. (The Hopi wind deity — called *Yaponcha* — is still associated with the place of volcanoes northeast of Sedona.) Life improved and the Sinagua began building small structures of mud and stone for food storage and field shelters. Larger stone structures were serving as homes by about 1100.

The pit house concept evolved into an underground ceremonial chamber known today as a kiva. A ladder or notched pole through the central smoke hole is the only entrance into a kiva, guaranteeing privacy for the men weaving textiles and preparing for ceremonies. It is here that Sinaguan and Hopi boys have been initiated into the men's secret societies.

Over time, the Sinagua occupied territory from what is

Left, a Sinagua ruin (upper right area of photo) mentioned in this chapter remains concealed in the Red Rock-Secret Mountain Wilderness Area. Sinaguans may have chosen such an inaccessible site to deter raiders, provide weather protection, or simply preserve space for crops.

Above, Sinagua Indians once lived in what now is Walnut Canyon National Monument, northeast of Sedona.

now Wupatki National Monument in the north down to Montezuma Castle National Monument in the south, from Sycamore Canyon and Tuzigoot National Monument in the west across to Clear Creek in the east. Many settlements, including those preserved in Walnut Canyon National Monument and Elden Pueblo, thrived at various times.

An ease of life peaked for the Sinagua from A.D. 1150-1250, and then the climate became increasingly cooler and drier as the rain patterns shifted. The people moved closer together to consolidate resources and began building larger pueblos.

JESSE WALTER FEWKES, an archaeologist working for the Smithsonian Institution, first visited Sedona in 1895 while studying Hopi and Zuni migration routes.

He documented two large structures in an alcove at the head of Red Canyon. He named the pueblo village *Palatki* (Puh-LOT-key), meaning "Red House" in the Hopi language. In the eastern half of the alcove, a well-preserved nine-room dwelling, once standing two stories high, had been occupied in the 12th and 13th centuries. The alcove's west end contains a five-room dwelling with a kiva. Nearby, a spring once flowed into a large catch basin. Several eras of rock art have been painted and inscribed along the surrounding cliff walls.

For a larger ruin northwest of Palatki and from the same period, Fewkes chose Honanki (Hoe-NON-key) to mean "Bear House" in recognition of nearby bear habitat. (It since has been

noted that the name actually translates to Badger House.)

In the final days of the southern Sinagua, the people built large pueblo communities next to the rivers, streams, and permanent water sources here in the Verde Valley. Every 2 miles up Beaver Creek was yet another pueblo. Drought had set in across the Southwest. Individual communities began defining their territories with fortified lookouts located on promontories. Territorial boundaries may have been enforced to ensure dependable resources for each community.

On an autumn day in 1582, Spanish explorer Antonio de Espejo and four companions rode horses down through Oak Creek Canyon into the Verde Valley. They found the magnificent, yet abandoned villages. The Sinagua had been gone for well over a century. Crossing the Rio de los Reyes, now known as the Verde River, Espejo's band headed toward the ancient mine in what is now Jerome. At the mine they found copper but wanted silver, and so they rode on.

The Yavapai (People of the Sun) were living near Sedona when the Spanish arrived. They spoke a Yuman dialect and are related to the Havasupai (People of the Blue-Green Water) in the Grand Canyon. Did the Sinagua and Yavapai co-exist for a time? Did some of the Sinagua stay behind and revert to older practices? Did intermarriage happen among these tribes of different languages? Each is a strong possibility, and archaeologists likely will give you different answers.

But why would the Sinagua choose to leave a place with a steadily flowing river, good farmlands, and a mild climate? Many possibilities exist: devastation of a long-term drought; disease from living in large communities; depletion of resources; destiny to keep on their mythological path.

THE LAST DOORWAY in the ancient dwelling awaits me. Wood lintels, each about 2 inches thick, support the low doorway. Smoke-darkened bark clings to the wood. Avoiding contact with the stone or wood, I crawl through the centuries-old passageway into darkness. Crouching uncomfortably to avoid banging my head, I turn on my small flashlight and look around. The tiny light beam finds nothing inside the dark, deep chamber. Nothing except a large spider. It slowly crawls toward me across the low ceiling.

I make my way out, going under the low doorway and back into sunlight. My eyes strain, painful as they adjust. But the light is a welcome relief.

Kathleen has discovered agave quids, corncobs, and a piece of old bone on the dwelling floor. I try to forget the spider as I look at the bone fragment and its dry, exposed cells. It is very old and weighs next to nothing. Is it an animal bone? Human? Does it matter as it returns to earth?

I recall that 11th-century Chinese artist Kuo Hsi wrote, "There are landscapes in which one can travel, landscapes in which one may gaze, landscapes in which one may ramble, and landscapes in which one may dwell." Looking out again, into the canyon world below, I realize that at one time or another this land of red rocks has been all of these, and maybe more.

Nourishment
[JOURNAL ENTRY]
June 20

STOPPING UNDER A cluster of trees along the Fay Canyon trail, I pull off my hat. I drink from my water bottle and use the hat to wipe my forehead. Sweat already has soaked through the hatband.

The tangy scent of sandstone and trees and bone-dry earth floats in the air. One day soon, tropical rainstorms will burst onto the land. Until then, this effusive heat closes in hard and bright. As I recharge myself, a scratching sound starts from the underbrush as a slender lizard scurries into the sunlight.

Gold pinstripes streak the black from its head to its long, thin tail. It's a whiptail lizard. She quickly stops but doesn't stay put for long. Lifting up her midsection, she races — almost on tiptoes — across a long stretch of hot sand. Then, just as quickly, she stops beneath a manzanita bush, in a shadow as thin as a woman's wrist. Lining up her body within the long shadow, she finds shelter from the sun.

This desert grassland whiptail comes from — amazingly — an all-female species. And according to field guide authors Jonathan and Roseann Beggy Hanson, seven of the other 12 whiptail species in the Southwest engage in parthenogenetic reproduction: creating the next generation without the need of a partner or more literally through *virgin* birth. A typical desert grassland whiptail lays a clutch of one to four eggs that will hatch in 50 to 55 days.

The lizard before me scurries to a new place, noisily rummages around, and finds something to eat, probably an insect hiding under the duff of dry leaves. Suddenly she lifts herself into a push-up position and glares at me.

I hadn't moved. Did she feel my presence? Hear my thoughts? Sense my eyes upon her? I can't really know, but I silently send her a message. *You're beautiful.* She looks me directly in the eye. Should she trust me? She's not sure.

Again, I talk to her in my mind. *I won't hurt you, little one. I'm only curious to see what's going on in your world.* Our eyes lock on each other for a few moments longer. Then, she hurries away, deciding the hunt for food is more important.

Traveling deeper into the canyon, I reach a fork in the trail. Here, a jutting sandstone formation divides the canyon into two. I turn into the side canyon I haven't been to before. A narrow path eventually goes over exposed tree roots and zigzags higher and higher until it reaches a peach-colored shelf of rock. A ledge curving to the left goes under long, black and white mineral stains, a memory of water. Today, there is no waterfall mist to cool me. Instead, I endure an oven-hot cliff wall as I quickly walk by.

The path guides me to a shaded stone overhang and suddenly back into the sun. And there the path abruptly ends at a ledge. Sheer cliffs, like the prow of a tall sailing ship, fall away on both sides. This flat-rock deck of cross-bedded sandstone would be a nice place to sit and get to know this intimate canyon. Just not today. I turn away from the full-on exposure of the beating sun, heading back toward the comfort of shade. My foot knocks a slab of stone. Almost immediately, from across the canyon, I hear a strange sound. I look up and see nothing. The sound was the canyon echoing back to me.

Where the gracefully curving overhang blocks the sun I set down my daypack and sit. Feeling playful, I begin bouncing different sounds — whistling, singing, and then drumming on my thighs. This canyon's hidden charm makes me smile.

I begin to notice a slow gathering of silence. It is comforting in this modern world to feel the stillness — like being under a warm blanket on a cool evening. I settle in to wait out the midday heat and enjoy a simple lunch.

After awhile, my awareness drifts out of focus and drowsiness sets in. A flying insect quietly purrs by unseen. Distant birds send soft chirps floating through the calm air.

Then everything gently slides away. I awaken, sometime later, feeling peaceful and restored. The heat of the day has passed and I decide to explore.

Searching for higher ground, I spot a steep gully showing adventurous possibilities. The passage becomes narrow. Wedging my hands into small gaps, I search out places for my feet. After a few more awkward maneuvers, I reach another overhanging ledge and follow it deeper into clefts of the strangely eroded chamber.

Wondering what the thunderheads are up to, I move around a corner for a view of the horizon — and stop cold. Before me is an ancient room built of stones. Here, centuries ago, someone made this place home. My spirit soars from this surprise discovery.

As I quietly enter through the doorway, I'm aware of the feeling of being in someone else's home. I am a guest.

From inside the room, the view looking into the box canyon reveals dark, dry mineral stains of accumulated waterfalls streaking the cliffs. It probably won't happen today

— still too early in the summer — but when these waterfalls flow it must be something to behold. I call this place Waterfall House.

Something in the shadows catches my eye. A corncob. Its kernels had nourished the people of this ancient home. Now it's a reminder of lives already spent. It is a small remnant, yet it is also a living story. I leave the artifact where it is. All living things need nourishment, even a story. ☉

Opposite, a terrace covered by a natural overhang in the cliffs of Fay Canyon sheltered occupants from both winter rain and intense summer sun.

These cobs, above, came from corn grown by ancient farmers, who planted a variety of crops in canyon floors and open valleys.

Stenciled hand shapes of adults and children line up in rows in a remote cave in Dry Creek Basin. Their creators sprayed charcoal pigment over their extended fingers.

Drums of Life

[JOURNAL ENTRY]

August 30

WANDERING BIRD'S FEET have made a delicate linked-chain pattern in the fine sand covering the cave floor. A fox — or was it a ringtail? — left behind dance-step diagrams with its padded feet. And a snake has written his message with single-stroke calligraphy. Scattered rock rubble is interspersed among the animal tracks. A few old potsherds hide in the dust.

The air outside the cave is strangely calm. The sky is a muddy mixture of watercolors. Greenish-gray light hangs in the air.

From the cave's back wall, human hands begin to emerge. The ghostly shapes on the stone were made hundreds of years ago when people blew pigment over their hands. Many of the stenciled hand shapes are in rows. Adult hands, fingers spread wide. Little hands, those of children. And a mysterious, six-fingered hand.

The shapes of their hands were the marks they chose to leave. What signs of life will *we* leave? What will be *our* mark on the land?

Outside the cave, the natural sandstone is bare except for a pale ring around an evaporated rain pool. A wasp erratically patrols the dry spot. Maybe it remembers this water source, here, perhaps, only days before. Buried in the sand is another potsherd. A piece of a broken water jug?

Suddenly, a woodpecker rattles the forest. A scrub jay squawks and flies off. A bright, quick flash lights up everything. And then, the loud boom of thunder echoing back and forth fills the canyon. The air cools in a rush as the storm races in. Maybe once again, the small catch basin will quench the thirst of the many beating drums of life that pass this way. As the sky quickly changes, I move back inside to watch and wait out the storm.

The Snake

[JOURNAL ENTRY]

December 13

DEEP IN THE forested canyon our group of 20 or so gathers inside a long, shadowy alcove. We include a retired fighter pilot, a former schoolteacher, a handyman, a geologist, a writer, and a handful of retired engineers. We are all members of the Verde Valley Archaeology Society, and our group has made arrangements to visit this privately owned canyon outside of Sedona.

Our host, Matthew, a tall, sturdy man, explained before we hiked here, that Hartwell Canyon is owned by the Nature Conservancy. Matthew and his equally tall wife are the on-site caretakers, and they only occasionally host groups like ours. The rest of the time is theirs to be left alone.

Painted on the alcove's back wall, a nearly 15-foot-long plumed serpent exudes a commanding presence. As everyone takes it in, Matthew tells us the serpent has presided here for around 40 generations, perhaps 800 years.

Reminiscent of plumed serpent images from Central America and Mexico, the pictograph artist painted two enclosed circular bands, one black, and the other white, forming the head. Symbolic feathers were rendered as palm-sized triangles above and below the head with a third plume over its neck.

Matthew tells us the pictograph was painted with hand-ground pigments. White from kaolin clay or calcite. Black from charcoal. And reddish-brown from a mineral such as hematite. The snake was rendered with precision — geometric shapes all have clean, sharp edges; corners are exact; the execution was very purposeful.

A long row of interlocking triangles, painted light gray, each about 2 feet tall, completes the massive serpent body. A natural seep has left gray mineral stains over the midsection. The tail, that of a rattlesnake, is painted in a grid pattern of reddish-brown solid squares. The rattles are deliberately rendered as broken from the body.

Matthew decides to share a story about the day that he brought his father here. His father sat on the ground near the snake glyph and meditated. In a vision he saw three men, old and thin, squatting around a small fire in the alcove. Since once plentiful springs were drying up, they had come for knowledge and guidance from the snake.

Before Matthew finishes his talk, he points out that there are no other rock art symbols in the alcove except a series of small reddish-brown hatch marks, which might have designated water allotments for groups or clans living here. After he answers a few questions, we wander about to explore the alcove on our own.

Several of us walk up to the glyph to examine it more closely. We can't help but ponder its mysteries. In our culture, we are told the serpent is the villain. Because of the serpent, we all fell from grace in the Garden of Eden myth.

Our discussion delves into examples of serpent mythology.

Someone recently read that early cultural beliefs centered on bears and snakes because the animals hibernated. Awakening in spring,

A black-tailed rattlesnake sips water from a natural spring in the Grotto Alcove of Red Canyon. Some people consider this species to be the most attractive and least aggressive of rattlesnakes.

the animals symbolized life coming back after death. Joseph Campbell wrote about early people seeing the snake shed its skin as a sign of it being born again. In Kundalini yoga, a serpent traveling up through the seven chakras symbolizes the uncoiling of spiritual energy. Someone else adds that a snake climbs the staff of Aesculapius, the Greco-Roman god of healing and medicine — the symbol used by the American Medical Association.

Bringing us closer to home, another person mentions the prominence of the snake in symbols and mythology of the Hopi Indians of northern Arizona. There is the ancient story of Tiyo. It is said this young Hopi man was the first person to float down the Colorado River through the Grand Canyon. Returning from his "hero's journey" he brought the Snake Dance ceremony to his people.

The myth tells how on the long journey he fell in love with a beautiful, young woman. Tiyo soon asked her father's approval to marry her. Her father was the snake priest and decided to test young Tiyo by surrounding him with hissing rattlesnakes. Tiyo showed great courage during the test. He won the father's approval. For a wedding gift her father taught Tiyo an especially sacred ceremony. When Tiyo took his bride home, he taught the Snake Dance ceremony to his people.

None of us has ever witnessed this secretive ceremony still held on the Hopi mesas. After talking about snake legends, we realize that most serpent mythology is beneficial, except in Western culture.

Sinaguan petroglyphs of animals, or *zoomorphs*, often were rendered near or along a natural crack in the rock. Yavapai traditionalists believe in spirits that they call the "small people." These spiritual beings live beyond the stone, through the cracks, inside the Earth. The snake is said to be a messenger to this spirit world. Interestingly enough, the concept of "heaven" for the Yavapai is not up in the sky, but down inside the Earth.

In our own urban culture, the rattlesnake almost always conjures up fear. The fangs, the buzzing tail, the toxic venom — they all scare us. Is the rattlesnake's intent really evil? Probably not. He wants to not get hurt and maybe to just be left alone. The philosopher of our group asks, "Is fear not

the threshold keeping us from accessing our deepest well of consciousness?"

Along with a few others, he and I decide to head off and explore the rest of the alcove. As it leads down canyon, we round a corner and come upon a beautiful bowl-shaped area of solid stone. The natural amphitheater amplifies our voices and footsteps. I whistle to entice music from the rock.

I walk to the deepest part of the echoing side canyon and find a 30-foot vertical sandstone seep glistening with moisture. Bright green moss clings to the tall, wet rock and tender maidenhair fern wavers in the air. How can we not love this beautiful Earth that gives us life?

"Do you remember the ancient Greek myth of Echo?" John asks.

I tell him no, I don't think I've heard it.

"Echo was this beautiful, young nymph who lived and played in a forest near the stream. She was one of Gaia's daughters, the great goddess of the Earth. I like to think of Echo, in this story, as symbolizing Nature.

"So anyway, one day a handsome, older boy happens to stroll by. Think of him, perhaps, as symbolizing modern man. So the good-looking chap stops and flirts with Echo, and she thinks he is actually attracted to her. He is so handsome she can't help but immediately fall in love with him. But sadly, Echo tries everything to win him over, and no matter what she does, he scorns her.

"The young man was really very self-centered — only interested in himself — and had flirted with her just for his own entertainment. But she never did give up wanting his love. But as time slipped on, she ever so slowly wasted away, eventually turning to stone. And now, the only part of Echo that remains alive is her voice in the stone still calling for his love.

"And who was this selfish boy?" John asks. "His name was none other than Narcissus."

After we all regroup in the alcove and begin the hike to our vehicles, I remember that today is Sunday. It feels like church service is over. I say goodbye to the others as we re-enter our everyday lives, each of us carrying home the deep memories of our soul. ☾

Winter Sun

[JOURNAL ENTRY]

December 21

A CALM SILENCE prevails as I walk into Red Canyon toward Palatki ruin. The low, winter sun glows through dry grass standing tall between prickly pear cactus and scrub oak. Rust cliffs rise on three sides, each memorializing water runoff with bold, black strokes. Only occasionally do the long, vertical stripes shine wet. Those are special days, exciting to behold.

A movement interrupts a memory of one of those days. On a leafless branch, high up in a mesquite tree, perches a sleek, elegant little bird, black as coal, with a sporty little head crest. Its reddish-orange eye looks at me, then away. A subtle green shines iridescent from its black feathers as if reflecting the nearby oak trees. Slowly raising its head crest, the phainopepla shyly chirps. After picking a few more mistletoe berries, it flies away, small white feather patches flashing with each wing beat.

Over the top of the oak trees I see the alcove below the cliff. Inside — protected — is Palatki, a small village of dwellings built from native stones by the Sinagua people at the same time that Europe was building castles. The modern-day Hopi, the descendants of the ancient Sinagua, believe Palatki is not abandoned. To them, it is still a home, now melting back into the Earth from where it came.

I pause a moment, remembering the Ancient Ones. With respect, I enter the central room by stepping under the low, exterior doorway. I have come, once again, to a place where the ancient people worked and played, worried, laughed, and loved.

Today is one of the special occasions they would have celebrated. The daily southward

Indians rendered this pictograph panel, above, using mineral pigments to depict animals and humans, including a figure with a hunting bow. The tall human figure is believed to be a shaman with sacred datura seedpods hanging from his ears. The rock art is located on the Woo Ranch, bounded by the Red Rock-Secret Mountain Wilderness.

At right, Palatki ruin lies in a sunny alcove. Palatki's community was active until the beginning of the 14th century.

Opposite, the Big Dipper, a small portion of the Ursa Major constellation, hovers over Bear Mountain near Boynton Pass.

movement of the points where the sun rises and sets now pauses before reversing direction. Winter solstice. On Christmas, four days from now, the sun's northward migration begins. For the next six months, with each subsequent sunrise, the light will return to stay a few minutes longer each day.

Indian calendars record important days by where the sun rises in relation to landmarks on the horizon. Vernal equinox. Summer solstice. Autumnal equinox. Winter solstice. Each is three moon cycles apart from the next one, and many of the holidays on our modern calendar still relate to these natural phenomena.

Only at winter solstice does the light of sunset enter Palatki by reaching around the cliffs enclosing Red Canyon. For those Sinagua families who lived here in the 12th and 13th centuries, these special few sunsets would have glazed their home in brilliant amber and light rose, the same as now.

As the brilliant light slowly fades, Mingus Mountain, far away on the horizon, turns purple and blue with a brilliant glow behind it. High overhead, the sky is a rich blue, the same as a deep-blue mountain lake. The color only hints at the infinite depth of space.

High overhead, a raven pair sails over fading landforms. The rollicking ravens

have returned home for the night. Their conversation echoes off the cliff walls.

The first stars poke through the darkening sky. I leave the alcove and walk back down the trail, under the dark forest canopy, past the rock garden of standing stones, and out into the open. Cold night air sinks onto the land as more and more stars shimmer above. First Orion shows up. Then the Big Dipper. And finally the Seven Sisters of Pleiades. They all sparkle and shine. This is their longest night to celebrate the clear, winter sky. ◌

Chapter 2

Raven and Coyote

I think of the millions of bones that have fallen to earth — bones like sticks of hail, melted into the earth, nourishing it.

— Mark Spragg, *Where Rivers Change Direction*

A RAVEN, PERCHED ON A LEDGE of red rock, turns and looks in my direction. Warm spring wind lifts its neck feathers, revealing fluffy white down underneath. I have scrambled up into its domain. Looking to one side, I sink into a nonthreatening position. The bird turns its head like a castle guard and stares motionlessly straight ahead.

Apparently at ease, the raven issues melodic gurgles from deep in its throat. Stretching its neck and raising up its head, the creature finishes each stanza with a sharp clack by snapping shut its large beak. It looks very amused with itself.

Spreading its wings, it jumps wide open into the wind and hovers just beyond my reach. It turns and looks directly into my soul. Its eye gives a mischievous little glint. *Hey, human, bet you can't do this*, it seems to say just before it tucks down through air currents and sails away.

In the mesquite-covered flatlands below, finches, sparrows, and scrub jays flit about. The reddish house finches seem to be playing a game of musical chairs among the yucca stalks of summers gone by. Hummingbirds, desert bees, and orange-legged blister beetles will be attracted to this year's pale-green stalks once they begin to bloom.

Near where I am sitting grows a graceful piñon tree. The bottom arching trunk/branch is a complete complement to the upper trunk/branch. All of its limbs have fresh, young needles. From the tree's crown a golden-yellow bird with a jet-black head lets out a watery melody. This sprightly Scott's oriole is one of 180 bird species living around the Sedona area. The oriole continues singing.

Songbirds have several styles of vocal communication. Males sing long songs, like the joyful melody being whistled nearby, in hopes of attracting a mate. Short, repetitive calls are used to reinforce or establish claims to territory.

Open-field birds, like the house finches still playing below, use high-pitched notes in their songs and calls. These notes carry better over long, open spaces or through the wind. Birds living in the forest use lower, deeper notes — tones that carry better through dense foliage.

My red rock perch slowly submerges in shadow. Clouds in the aeolian sea above shine brightly with late-afternoon light. A purring rattle softly announces the presence of one of Sedona's smallest birds. The unique sound, made from the movement of specialized feathers, comes from a hummingbird.

Not having much of a voice, hummingbirds — such as the rufous or Anna's — must establish their territory with aggressive aerial displays. But male broad-tailed hummingbirds use a unique purring rattle in place of all that show-off nonsense. The hummer flies off just as two swifts — in fast pursuit of airborne insects — swish by at jet-fighter speed.

~⟡~

EVERYTHING SEEMS TO be enjoying this time between the dormancy of winter and the searing heat of mid-summer. Spring wildflowers grow scattered from the reddish soil among cactus, mesquite, and piñons. In shaded areas, penstemon call silently to hummingbirds with tall stems of scarlet flowers. Miniature purple blossoms decorate lacy, knee-high bushes of

On the preceding panel [pages 26 and 27], old agave stalks linger in an evergreen thicket, sharply contrasting with the stony cliffs of Munds Mountain.

Owls clover, left, accents Boynton Pass after being nurtured by a wet winter.

Above, a pair of ravens soar, and, right, the flowers of a strawberry hedgehog cactus signal that spring has arrived.

feather dalea. Blooming close to the ground, blackfoot daisies make clusters of bright white rosettes.

A variety of nectar seekers visit flowering yuccas, but only one visitor can actually pollinate the flower — a moth. The two exemplify a perfect symbiotic relationship — the yucca needs the moth, and the moth needs the yucca.

While inside the yucca's flower, the moth deliberately rolls sticky yucca pollen into a little ball and moves it onto the flower's stigma out on the end of the protruding pistil. Once the pollen ball is in place, the little moth vigorously pounds it down. This strange performance happens to be the only way to fertilize the flower — beginning its transformation into seed-bearing fruit.

Having completed this interesting act of pollination, the moth lays its eggs deep in the yucca flower. When the time is right, the eggs hatch and the surrounding yucca fruit becomes a ready supply of food. Some, but not all, of the yucca fruit gets eaten. Enough remains so the plant can spread its reproductive seeds to continue the survival of both species.

Agave — another drought-tolerant plant — is most often found in a small community like the one growing below me. One particular agave, perhaps several decades old, has chosen this to be the year it sacrifices its life to help ensure there will be another generation of its kind. The agave has rapidly grown its flower stalk, six or more inches each day. Now it yields

yellow blossoms tipped with red. The plant's energy quickly drains away as it goes to seed. Only the top of its asparagus-like stalk remains green; the ball of daggers is already withered and brown.

Ocotillo, plants with long and thorny wands clumped at the base, have sprouted a covering of fingernail-sized leaves since the last rainfall. After a few dry weeks, the leaves will blow away like yellow confetti only to grow back after the next rain. Using this opportunistic strategy allows the ocotillo to make a home in hot and dry niches ignored by less hardy plants.

THE TWO MOST important factors affecting what grows here in Sedona, or in any environment, are moisture availability and temperature tolerance. Elevation and slope angle help determine these factors. Higher elevations generally are cooler and wetter, and the same holds true for north-facing slopes.

Small trees, like the graceful piñon behind me, inhabit the Piñon-Juniper Woodland community, one of the five environmental life zones around Sedona, an area with more than 550 seed-producing wild plant species.

The diminutive evergreens of the Piñon-Juniper Woodland (P-J) cover much of the undisturbed natural areas in northern Arizona. Piñons seldom grow taller than 20 or 30 feet. Juniper trees, such as the Utah and one-seed juniper, live much longer, yet hardly ever grow as tall as the piñons. Together, P-J most

A common fence lizard, below, climbs about looking for insects to eat. The yucca, right, has tough fibers that Sinagua Indians once used for making durable sandals.

Opposite page, a piñon pine tree, wild grass, scrub oak, and prickly pear cactus share a slope on Bear Mountain.

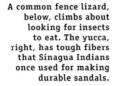

often fills the niche between 4,000 and 7,500 feet of elevation. Mule deer, or at least their tracks, can be spotted in this life zone among the yucca, agave, Mormon tea, fendlerbush, and the sweet-smelling cliffrose.

The P-J shares similar conditions with another community — the Chaparral. Both are found between the relatively cool and moist Ponderosa Pine-Fir life zone above them and the hotter, drier Desert-Grassland zone below. P-J prefers fine soil that holds moisture, while Chaparral thrives in areas with rocky, well-drained soil. A vast area of Chaparral can be seen on the escarpments east of State Route 89A in Oak Creek Canyon. Chaparral-covered slopes have dense thickets of manzanita, mountain mahogany, and prickly scrub oak — a frustrating combination for hikers.

The high country around the Mogollon Rim holds ideal conditions for the Ponderosa Pine-Fir life zone community. The soaring pines above Sedona mark the southern edge of the world's largest ponderosas forest. The tall trees usually grow in an elevation around 7,000 feet and higher, but a few pon-

derosas grow in lower-elevation side canyons. Douglas fir and Engelmann spruce appear in scattered pockets of damp soil. In open areas between stands of trees, you might see purple-blue lupine flowers and waist-high bracken ferns.

A solitary ponderosa on the northwest side of Mitten Ridge facing 89A has found just the right combination of shade and moisture. This low-elevation pioneer never receives direct sunlight, except for the few days when the setting sun is farthest north, and then only for an hour or two just before the sun sets. This lone pine silently marks our summer solstice.

Covering much of the southern and western sections of Red Rock Country are the desert grasses, such as sideoats gramma and black gramma. Plants of the Desert-Grassland community grow best in deep soil existing in places such as Boynton Pass between Doe Mesa and Bear Mountain. (Many native grasses were unfortunately overgrazed, shifting the balance in favor of mesquite, four-wing saltbush, and snakeweed.) Plants of the Desert-Grassland community that prefer more gravely soils are prickly pear, cholla, ocotillo, catclaw acacia, and beargrass.

Golden columbine, far left, blooms along Summers Spring in Sycamore Canyon. Ferns, above, flourish in the shade of West Fork Canyon. Awaiting twilight and the time to hunt, an owl tucks its head.

Opposite, Douglas fir and ponderosa pine trunks catch the late afternoon light on Secret Mountain.

A fifth major life zone, the Riparian community, fills out with golden columbine, wild grape, Virginia creeper, New Mexico raspberry, maidenhair fern, monkeyflower — and poison ivy — living in shady, damp places. These are the plants that need permanent water and live near it. Oak Creek Canyon and the many side canyons of the region support a variety of trees: Arizona alder, box elder, velvet ash, several varieties of oak, and West Fork's colorful fall favorite — the bigtooth maple. Riparian areas that receive more sunlight have larger trees such as Fremont cottonwood, Arizona walnut, and the Arizona sycamore with its bright white bark that peels into an army-camouflage pattern.

THE LATE AFTERNOON sun is coloring the land ever more brilliantly. Shadows are beginning their transition from blue into purple. Quail politely holler back and forth. After one last stammering call, all is noticeably silent.

A sharp, wild barking cuts the stillness. I look for the coyote from my perch, but it doesn't reveal itself or stop barking for what seems like minutes. Then, they appear — one, two, then a whole family. Excited, they jump and run about, their tails wagging furiously. The young coyotes nip and jostle each other. Then the evening hunt begins as the parents move out. The youngsters follow like shadows of smoke through the brush and scrub.

Coyotes are one of 250 vertebrate species (animals with a backbone) that biologists have recorded in the wilderness around Sedona. From javelinas, black bears, and mountain lions to rock squirrels, deer mice, and gray foxes, more than 60 percent of them depend on permanent water sources during some part of their life cycles. A dry year can raise havoc.

A RAVEN'S CAWING repeatedly echoes off the bluff behind me. Perhaps it's the castle guard heading home to the communal roost. Darkness is settling upon the land. Time now for owls, bats, and the other night creatures to survey their domain. I make my way down from the bluff.

"Perhaps one true gift of these canyons is that they become so deeply imprinted on the psyche that they can be invoked at will, bringing back their particular charge of serene energy whenever needed," writes Ann Zwinger in *Wind in the Rock*, a book about the wild lands of the Southwest. "Many of us need this wilderness as a place to listen to the quiet, to feel at home with ancient rhythms that are absent in city life...."

In the glowing twilight I couldn't agree more, although my legs are taking me back into the human life zone. Once again, I re-enter the humming drone — of automobiles, electricity, and modern living — with just a little more wilderness planted in my heart.

Listening to a Juniper

[JOURNAL ENTRY]

February 1

THE TRAIL ROUNDS a bend and opens out onto a broad bench of solid sandstone — one of a rising series of smoothly eroded terraces. Near the middle of the rock slope, I angle up and begin to climb. The view opens up behind me as I ascend from one terrace to the next. Finally, with the western horizon unobstructed, I look for a spot to wait for the sunset. Like a dog, I circle around and find a spot to settle down where the rounded sandstone makes a perfect backrest.

As my body sinks into the stone, I take in my surroundings. A twisted and gnarled juniper is established on the slope, making a life here. The tree has obviously survived for centuries. Its wide trunk divides upward into several large, flat branches. Each branch divides into smaller and smaller flame-like divisions. The thicker branches have soft strips of bark hanging down in torn shreds. Only a few branches end in clusters of living green. More often than not the bare branches appear dead.

Then I hear the old tree whisper, "Look into my life, and you will learn much."

"What can you tell me?" I wonder.

I have never talked to a tree before. But there are questions I have had for years.

"Old Juniper, I see your trunk and branches are often twisted in spirals. I have been curious: Does the wind make you grow this way?"

"No, not just the wind, although I must face its many moods. A spiral, I have learned, will not easily break. I grow this way for strength against the weight of wet snow, the impact of falling sandstone, and the push of the wind."

One of Juniper's thick and shaggy branches grows on the ground, reaching its horizontal bulk across the slope. On the uphill side the trunk stops a collection of rocky soil from eroding downhill. A sparse plant community grows in the dammed up soil.

"Since long ago, I have planned ahead. The summer rains run off the ground so quickly. After experiencing this, I had an inspiration. If I could slow down the runoff, my underground parts could have more to drink. So I grew a water dam. A way to make the most of what I was given."

"So you created a way to water yourself?"

"Indeed," wise Juniper replies. "I follow all possibilities of growth. Most trees want to be taller and taller. But they can't last. My kind grows to live a long life."

"To me, many of your branches appear to be dead. How do you survive?" I ask.

"When times are abundant, I grow. When I sense space available for growth, I evaluate my ability. My roots talk to my needles. I observe the wind and sun patterns. Will I be able to send life-giving moisture to a new branch? Can new needles gather the light without overusing resources? My roots seek cracks in the sandstone, places of hidden moisture, places to anchor against the wind.

"But when times are not as good, I reduce my flow. Then many of my branches may no longer show green. But I do not reject these parts of myself that are no longer growing. They are part of who I am, and they still support my life."

"How do your dead-looking branches still support life?"

"Oh, it is very simple," Juniper says. "My dead branches hold me. They shade me from the fierce sun. I can reduce my needs and survive drought. It all works out for the best."

"What would you like to happen around you? Do you want more water, better soil?

"I simply wish to watch the progress of the seasons. I like the summer sun and the winter cold. The position of the stars and the phases of the moon are my calendar. The cycles of the sun are my timepiece. I need nothing more. I am in no hurry to live my life. I am content to be as I am. I wish to be left unbroken by twilight fire builders and uncut by nature re-arrangers. I am old. I have learned to grow here, in this desert, because I am patient."

Then I notice old Juniper has a long branch with healthy green growth reaching out to a nearby piñon branch.

"We share our differences," the old tree volunteers. "The piñon shades the ground, and I trap the water. We help small, young plants spread their roots and get started. His thick needles give shelter. Young plants need a protected place to get a healthy start."

I notice baby prickly pear cactus and

Fresh snow dusts a centuries-old juniper at Soldiers Pass.

tiny ocotillo growing underneath the piñon's branches.

"Someday," old Juniper continues, "the piñon will have lived his life and his branches will no longer show green. But as he returns to the earth, he will make the soil richer — more complete. His decaying body will create a home for more life. On a dead branch, a hawk may wait for a passing meal. Another bird might build a nest in a small cavity. A pack rat will have sticks and twigs, brought down by the wind, to collect for her home. As the piñon dies, insects in his decaying trunk will feed woodpeckers and lizards. We are patient and content to do our part. We live at peace with life, and when we die we hope to leave this place better than when we arrived."

I can ask nothing more. ◯

Twilight Vision

DROPPING OVER THE rim from the sharp, tangy desert, the trail steeply enters Sycamore Canyon. With each step, the heat and dust fade. I begin to hear — rising faintly into the air — the burbling sounds of moving water.

Running clear and steady, Sycamore Creek waits at the bottom of the trail, a mile upstream from its confluence with the Verde River. The air becomes cool and moist as I enter the world shaded by sycamore and cottonwood trees. I start hiking upstream.

Trunks and branches of huge trees tower overhead with fresh leaves and sun-warmed bark. Around them, rich and damp soil adds a pleasant aroma to the air. A swallowtail butterfly silently glides toward me, holding its large, elegant wings motionless. With a flutter of sunflower yellow, it veers around me and continues downcanyon. I follow the flashing movement until the butterfly disappears among the desert cliffs. The receding, faded orange sandstone cliffs rise

high, holding back the sky. I walk farther up the canyon corridor. Grasses, shrubs, and wildflowers are bursting with moist energy. The downward-facing rows of bright-red penstemon flowers and the thimble-sized orange globemallow blossoms hang into the trail.

Following the trail about a mile and a half, I come to a less-traveled side route straying off under low tree branches and around bright green, twisting vines. The stray trail meanders without a clear destination. Then, an energetic and enchanting sound draws me to a private world. Here, a 3-foot wide, spring-fed channel of sparkling-clear water runs below a natural canopy in delicate shades of green.

Ducking around a small alder tree, I look up. Hiding in the cool shadows, an explosion of joyous, yellow fireworks — golden columbine, not five or ten but hundreds — grow on both sides of the channel. Flying over 3-foot high clouds of pastel green leaves, the columbines skyrocket every which way. Light filtering through the tree canopy spotlights the flowers with intermittent flashes. The scene resembles shooting stars and sends my spirit skyward.

When I head back, on another route to the main trail, wild and tender grape vines line the way. Tendrils spiral upward while vines search for new anchors to climb tree trunks and low-hanging branches. Hiding in the garlands of fresh, new leaves are clusters of young grapes no bigger than sesame seeds. The juicy, tart, wild grapes are still months from ripening for hungry birds and curious people.

Warming up their voices in slow, baritone repetitions — crooak . . . croak . . . crooooak — male frogs begin calling out from the shadows, sounding as if the effort was too much work. Maybe they are just pacing themselves; for evening is still young, and

it is safer, for sure, to wait until after dark before trying to entice the females. Then they can confidently let loose with all the frenzied, amphibian sexiness they can muster.

Twilight is cloaking the canyon as I return up the main trail. I stop to catch my breath and to look back. Above the riparian canopy, I see a great blue heron. Its silhouette silently glides through the blue, pink, and orange sky. Lifting slowly, the large bird moves along stroke by long stroke.

It has finished its day of stalking small fish, frogs, and salamanders. Now tucked away side by side, the heron's long chopstick legs extend backward. As it silently passes overhead, a gap shows on one of its broad wings, letting the twilight through where a feather should be. Its flight leads it to an overnight roost somewhere high above ground, away from sneaky, prowling, hungry coyotes.

Resuming the climb, I finally break over the rim of the canyon and re-enter the world of cactus and dust. The last colors drain out of the western sky. Standing in the twilight, I look back at the canyon now filled with shadow. High above, stars begin to flicker and shine, recalling for me the image of the golden columbine. ◯

Sycamore Creek, opposite, supports a variety of vegetation as it tumbles toward the Verde River west of Sedona. Also in Sycamore Canyon, above, Summers Spring slips past golden columbines.

A great blue heron, left, waits motionless while hunting for a small water creature to feed upon.

Rituals of Spring

[JOURNAL ENTRY]
May 13

THE SCATTERED WILDFLOWERS, including blackfoot daisies and feather dalea, look more fossilized than wilted from the sun. The southern slope of Mitten Ridge, here between Giant's Thumb and Teapot, is hot, dry, and completely still. So, the cedar gnats are out in force. I wish the little buzzing pests would quit crash landing in my eyes or flying up my nose.

A much louder buzzing intrudes — I immediately stop. Is it a swarm of wild bees? A coiled rattlesnake? Where? What is making that sound? Then I spot movement — a buzzing dark blur — a few feet above the ground over a low clump of manzanita. If it's an insect, then it's the biggest one I've ever seen. I stand, frozen, and watch. Finally, letting out a deep sigh, I recognize a harmless hummingbird.

The hummer flies a few feet horizontally, twists its tail almost 90 degrees, and flies back to where it started and repeats the pattern again and again. Without warning, it zooms straight up 30 feet, turns, and zips downward in an arcing path. It crosses over the spot where it was hovering and continues ascending in the same quick arc to the 30-foot height. It turns and makes another diving arc over the special center spot. I hear a purring chatter as it passes only a few feet above the ground.

This time I notice that when it reaches the 30-foot level it repositions clockwise. Scribing another arc, it seems to be drawing a basket shape in the air. After vertically tracing two more U-shaped ribs, its pattern brings it flying straight toward me! Its sharp beak, like a turbo-powered dart, passes only inches from my left shoulder. On its return pass it misses piercing me — by only inches — on my right shoulder. Now that it has my complete attention, the hummer abruptly goes off course to a dead piñon branch and lands.

Relieved at not being a jousting target any longer, I come to understand the situation. The bird's special someone must be sitting nearby. From his post he looks left,

then right, then left again, checking traffic. Wherever she is, I can't see her. Probably just as well. He seems to be the dangerous, jealous type.

For a few more minutes, I watch. Then, stumbling on the idea, I realize I'm standing in the middle of the dance floor. I turn to

leave while the pugnacious little hummingbird continues to try stirring up some romance. After all the effort he has put out with his daring aerial display, I wonder if the hidden female is interested. To me this cocky flying ace is just another show-off, but to her . . . well, maybe, he's the next Tom Cruise.

Ah, the timeless rituals of spring. ⟲

Singly, as the sunflower, above, or in groups such as the globemallow, larkspur, and bright red paintbrush dispersed among prickly pear, right, wildflowers bring a palette of colors to the outback and food for the hummingbird, above.

Early morning light paints the reflection of Coffeepot Rock onto the Seven Sacred Pools.

Sacred Life
[JOURNAL ENTRY]
July 13

AN HOUR BEFORE sunrise I awaken and look out the window with a sense that a lingering gloominess has passed. For days clouds have hung low, drifted through Soldiers Pass, hidden Wilson Mountain, and washed the land with the first summer rains. This morning I clearly see stars and quickly load up the van with camera gear. I know exactly where I want to be.

Driving eastward I see the sleepy sky waking up, blushing above the horizon. Taking a trail, I descend into the forest, finding the dawn air surprisingly warm. Tropical scents heavy with humidity float between the tree shapes. I wouldn't be surprised to discover dinosaurs grazing on treetops around the next bend. The damp, misty landscape seems ripe for magic.

Reaching a landmark sandstone outcropping, I detour off the trail. Here, filled to the brim, pools stair-step down sculpted sandstone. The clear liquid — just beginning to take on the colors of day — glistens in pockets carved in stone. I look into the pools, one after another. This place has been blessed as Seven Sacred Pools.

Approaching the largest, I see the storm debris of twigs and pine needles washed up on the sandstone shores. As I position my camera and tripod, I notice the smallest of movements in each pool. The summer rains have fashioned a home. As tadpoles propel themselves about the pool, the wiggling amphibians strike me as the symbol of childhood wonderment. What a transformation they will experience as they quickly change to hopping, jumping, full-grown frogs.

Clinging to the sandstone under a ledge, an adult frog hides. (Is this the mother of the squirming brood?) The canyon tree frog has the ability to quickly change its skin coloring to match its surroundings. In this case, pinkish-brown with gray mottling camouflages it from hungry raccoons, coyotes, and foxes. If one of these predators should get too close, the frog can easily jump into the water for safety.

As the morning brightens, clouds float upside down on the reflecting pools. First light begins stroking its colors — pink, then orange, and finally yellow. Then, the towering cliffs above Soldiers Pass begin glowing. I work the camera and adjust the shutter speed to match the increasing light.

The tadpoles continue to dapple faint concentric rings in the shining pools. Golden light slowly sweeps into the valley and down to the sandstone outcropping, baptizing the pools, one at a time, in beautiful morning colors. With a new generation of life swimming about, the moment is sacred indeed.

The Return Visit

[JOURNAL ENTRY]
November 2

STEERING HIS BIG Chevy van down Oak Creek Canyon, artist Michael Coleman casually pointed out a small side canyon.

"Good fall color up in there," he said as we headed into another sweeping curve.

A few hours earlier we had departed from the Grand Canyon, heading home after a nine-day river trip. We were almost back to Sedona when he decided to share this secret. As it turns out, I had driven by this place dozens of times, never knowing what was tucked away from view.

Days later, Kathleen and I drove to the spot to make our first pilgrimage into the hidden side canyon. Here, good soil, just enough water, and a favorable amount of sunlight had produced a dense population of autumn-ripe maples. Overhead, each leaf shimmered scarlet or tangerine or sunflower yellow, casting its radiant glow into the heavenly air.

Today, Earth having once again circled the sun, it's one year later. This time I walk into the small canyon alone. Remembering the bright, colorful leaves and ultramarine sky, I wonder if this place could ever be more than that memory.

The moment I step out of the van I tune into the sound of moving water coming from the side canyon. Earlier this week, a series of wet storms finally broke up. The weather people tell us we had 5 inches of precipitation this past month. We usually get one.

I walk into the roadside forest and within minutes forget about time. The canyon's creek bed — usually dry and silent — is now a flowing mountain stream surrounded by amazingly colorful maples. Curving and shining, tumbling and splashing,

A seasonal stream flows through an intimate side canyon laced with autumn-gold maples in Oak Creek Canyon.

the clear, ephemeral stream sparkles and echoes. It is truly a gift. Running water wasn't here a month ago, and by next week it may be gone.

But this is only the beginning. Last week's rain pulled leaf after leaf from the delicate branches. They cover the ground like a layer of party confetti, rich and vibrant in color.

Dividing all the color, the dancing stream slips around one protruding rock and then another. Over cobbles and boulders, I explore further upstream. Bright yellow leaves congregate on the surface of a spinning pool. Orange leaves cling to wet boulders. Clear water cascades over waist-high waterfalls. All along the way, the shoreline is carpeted with leaves. Leaves of orange transition into yellow. Violet and crimson leaves appear around the next bend. Still further, it's all yellow leaves once again.

Exiting the streambed, I follow a faint game trail. Reaching a shelf of the forest floor, I peer down from the path through a screen of branches and see the creek glinting white sparks.

Then the way becomes tangled in a maze of pines. The trail disappears under storm-shattered trees lying every which way on each other. I step cautiously over the slippery tree trunks, ducking and twisting around thick branches, and come into a small clearing. Just ahead, waiting, is a story that sends shivers under my damp clothing.

Below a young maple lies a large backbone broken in two. I scan the area. More bones. Scattered about my feet is a rotted shag carpet of brown hair. Short distances from the backbone are several curved ribs and an entire leg stripped of flesh; only hair clings above a cloven foot. My senses quicken. This is mountain lion territory. And bones are all that remain of this elk.

Standing water must have beckoned the thirsty and magnificent animal down from the rim to the stream one evening.

In the twilight, moving slowly, pausing, creeping, the lion stalked its prey.

The elk ambled through the velvety darkness down the game trail it remembered from before. Where the broken trees blocked its path it hesitated. And the mountain

lion pounced, slamming into the elk. Sharp claws ripped deep into flesh. Long fangs dug powerfully into the elk's neck, prying between vertebrae. Then, in a sudden jerk, the lion severed the spinal cord. With the warmth of life still inside it, the elk slumped into death.

The excited lion tore open the belly and devoured the heart, liver, and kidneys — organs rich in nutrients. Blood smeared its tawny face. Fierceness shone in its wild eyes. The cat ate the elk until completely satisfied. Then, learning of the kill, came hungry, scavenging ravens and coyotes. The festive colors of this autumn day hide the terrible cruelty that exists in life.

I wonder if maybe the colorful display of autumn leaves isn't a warning: "Beware — winter weather ahead." But whatever its purpose, the colorful display soon will fade. The leaves on the ground will begin to decay. Their once-living tissue will compost into soil. Soil filled with nutrients. Soil ready to hold moisture. Soil for the continuation of ripeness and return. ☉

Bright red and yellow maples, opposite, reflect across a placid pool signaling that it is autumn in West Fork Canyon.

Although deer, above, are seldom encountered, their tracks prove that their passage is not uncommon throughout Red Rock Country.

Maple trees splash color along the West Fork of Oak Creek.

The end of a rainbow, following panel [pages 44 and 45], touches the horizon above Mitten Ridge in the late afternoon.

Water Songs

Chapter 3

From the seeds the gourds grow,
Tended all summer by the water bearer,
Harvested in the fall:
Vessels to call the thunder home.

—William Eaton, *Water Bearer*

IN THE ARID WEST, HAVING enough water has always been a paramount issue, for water is the element most necessary to the health of people and land.

"Nowhere is water so beautiful as in the desert, for nowhere is it so scarce," noted Edward Abbey in *Beyond the Wall*, a collection of his writings and lectures based on hikes and other trips in the desert.

To at least some degree, parts of Arizona depend on saving water from snowmelt or rainfall in reservoirs for later use. Elsewhere, recycled water stretches the value of the relatively small amount of precipitation in this dry land. And 95 miles northeast of Sedona, an intensely religious ceremony continues each year to ask for the nurturing gift of rain. In August, high on the Hopi mesas, the Indians dance through "an elaborate series of prayers" in one of their 1,000-year-old village plazas. This sacred ritual is the famous Snake Dance (closed to the public).

Basically, Arizona has two seasons of precipitation — the summer monsoons and the winter snows in the high country and rain in the lower areas. Navajo Indians refer to the summer and winter rains by gender. In winter, Female Rain brings fog and mist. In summer, Male Rain storms onto the land.

People who have made the American Southwest their home speak with both awe and respect about summer monsoons. It is usually the hottest, wettest, and most dramatic time of the year. The sun bakes hot by the end of June. Eyes squint toward the horizon, searching for signs of a rising thunderhead. Locals make bets on what day the first monsoon will hit. But the heat continues, until finally, creeping up over the edge of the land come huge bright-white clouds with the movement of time-lapse photography. Massive cauliflower-shaped clouds swell upwards.

By mid-afternoon — if rain is coming — the bright clouds are already turning dark and angry. They start to smolder, heavy with anticipation. Lightning sears the increasing darkness. Rock-and-roll thunder rumbles over the land. More lightning flashes. Tension builds. The storm is rushing in. You soon smell the scent of rain, warning of what's to come, on the cool breath of the storm. Lightning rips apart the sky, and the rain explodes down on you. Bone-shaking thunder pounds your eardrums as the hard rain lashes and beats the land.

These savage storms originate with tropical moisture gathered over the Pacific Ocean off the coast of Mexico. The hot, sun-baked desert basins of the Southwest attract the cool, moist air northward. The atmospheric vacuum of a low-pressure system draws it in. Rain from these storms can fill canyon washes in no time. On a hike near Sugarloaf, I watched as the route across a dry streambed became submerged under a rushing, muddy torrent. It knocked large cobbles and stones against each other like bowling balls.

The fury can just as quickly pass with raindrops still splattering here and there. The sun re-emerges, and light moves in slow motion, rolling across the landscape. The cliffs begin to glow, and in a gesture asking forgiveness, a passing storm may leave a beautiful and radiant gift of a rainbow reaching down across the sky.

Sedona averages about 17 inches of rain each year. Some months may see no precipitation at all. In one recent summer, Red Rock Country endured a spell of more than 100 hot days without a drop of rain. Animals came out of the dry wilderness — desperate for water. Ponderosa and piñon trees struggled

Oak Creek, left, tumbles between boulders of water-polished basalt. As the creek descends through 15-mile long Oak Creek Canyon, it is fed by several natural springs including Sterling Springs at the head of the canyon. Above, Oak Creek spills over a ledge.

and many died. Withering orange leaves hung on manzanita branches. Parched cacti barely bloomed.

Another season, in another year, and Sedona seems more like coastal Oregon than desert. Clouds hang low for days; fog plays on the mesas and visits the valleys. Wet and glistening red rock reflects the sky while birds drink from waterholes. Clear water trickles down washes, and ephemeral water-falls play melodies in the canyons. The misty rains of November through March usually give their moisture in a gentle fashion, nurturing plants with long, slow drinks. Following a different pattern than the summer monsoons, these winter storms blow in from the Pacific Ocean and across the coast of California.

Waking up to see the red rocks and junipers dusted in white brings a special joy to many of us. In the shadows of Oak Creek Canyon, the average year can bring about 44 inches of snow. In town, Sedona's yearly average of snowfall is just shy of 9 inches.

In 1949, the month of January had record snows — repeated storms left 40 inches on Sedona.

The snow level often doesn't go lower than 5,000 feet — about the elevation of Slide Rock State Park in Oak Creek Canyon. Snow remains in shady canyons and on surrounding high points for a few days, or some-times weeks, and then melts. The snowmelt soaks slowly into the soil, its moisture encouraging spring wildflowers and helping replenish the underground aquifers.

Moisture-laden clouds, opposite top, dwarf the Sedona landscape. The monsoon clouds are formed after tropical air enters Arizona from Mexico's Pacific Coast and the dry desert heat sends it upward.

Snowmelt, opposite below, from the 12,633-foot-tall San Francisco Peaks, 35 miles north of Sedona, percolates into the porous volcanic soil before resurfacing at springs in Oak Creek Canyon.

Water cascades, above, in a series of falls in the normally dry wash of Bear Wallow Canyon on Schnebly Hill.

The highest point in Arizona is Humphreys Peak at 12,633 feet in the San Francisco Peaks, just 35 miles north of Sedona. Rising into the sky, the huge mountain attracts its own weather, amassing over 200 inches of snowfall in an average year. But come spring, there are surprisingly no mountain streams or small mountain lakes. Instead, because the San Francisco Peaks are the remnant of an ancient volcano, the water percolates through its porous cinders and cracks in its basalt.

This water does eventually resurface — in the form of springs. One such spring, located in a dark and forested ravine below the State Route 89A switchbacks, marks the beginning of Oak Creek. Sterling Springs fish hatchery utilizes water fresh from this spring for raising trout.

Another spring in Oak Creek Canyon is on the west side of the highway at Pine Flats Campground. This spring has been tapped, and you can fill your water bottles here, anytime, for free. At first glance it may look like someone left the faucet running at full volume. Don't worry, this is the spring's natural flow. What isn't used by roadside travelers runs harmlessly down into Oak Creek.

Oak Creek flows southward for its first 15 miles through Oak Creek Canyon. Along the way more babbling springs add to its volume. Deer, javelina, raccoon, skunk, coyote, and fox visit along the shores after twilight to safely quench their thirst. In the morning, look for their tracks. Birds are abundant here, nesting in the seasonal canopy of sycamore, oak, cottonwood, and alder.

Water from Oak Creek helped get Sedona on the map with another type of tree. Using waterwheels and gravity-fed flumes, pioneer families raised apples by diverting water from the creek to their orchards. In the late 1800s and early 1900s, the markets in Jerome, Prescott, and Flagstaff welcomed apples and fresh vegetables grown near Oak Creek.

In fact, during the Apache Indian wars, soldiers stationed

Waterfalls, such as this one in Boynton Canyon, left, may last less than an hour as sandstone shelves and terraces rapidly shed rainfall.

Wet Beaver Creek, above, flows year-around in the southeast corner of Red Rock Country. After passing through wilderness and then over red rock beside the Bell Trail, it continues past Montezuma Castle until eventually joining the Verde River.

at Fort Verde called this region Camp Garden.

Several streams other than Oak Creek flow year-round in the red rocks. West Fork, a small stream running through one of the most beautiful side canyons in Arizona, joins Oak Creek 10 miles upstream from Sedona. To the west is rugged Sycamore Canyon. Here, seasonal water aggressively rushes during spring snowmelt. During the rest of the year Sycamore Creek begins from Parsons Spring, gaining water from Summers Spring, peacefully cascading 4 miles to the Verde River.

To the south flows the year-round Wet Beaver Creek. Its cousin, Dry Beaver Creek, is seasonal. Seven hundred years ago, Sinagua Indians built pueblos close to Wet Beaver Creek

— including Montezuma's Castle — and farmed nearby cornfields. They chiseled glyphs of water birds and turtles into the red rock at what is now the V-Bar-V Petroglyph Site. (This site is the largest petroglyph panel in the Verde Valley and is open to the public.)

Oak Creek, Sycamore Creek, and Wet Beaver Creek empty into the Verde River. In the days before dams, the Verde flowed unchecked to the Salt River southeast of the McDowell Mountains. The Salt then flowed to the Gila just west of Phoenix, and the Gila flowed to the Colorado at Yuma, Arizona.

Creek water once flowed all the way to the Pacific Ocean. Now it gets diverted for agricultural, household, and recreational uses, or just plain evaporates before ever reaching the Sea of Cortes in Mexico.

Blanket of Life

[JOURNAL ENTRY]
January 4

FLOATING DOWN PIECE by tattered piece, the winter sky quietly descends in a slow, steady rhythm. The lazy, soft flow of the snow slowly hypnotizes me. Into the rhythm of its movement I walk along Thunder Mountain Trail below Capitol Butte. I'm surrounded by an elegant hush in a dreamy white landscape. Blinking, I look through the gauzy scene, and cliff formations begin appearing. Clouds drift, and a wash of warm light appears. Traveling slowly across the landscape, the glow sinks into Soldiers Pass. I continue walking.

Downy white pillows rest on evergreen boughs and cactus pads and cast shadows of robin's egg blue. Sunlight emerges from a hole in the white sky. Coffeepot Rock brightens as the fog lifts, and the sunlight reveals more and more ledges and cliff terraces detailed in white.

A quiet flutter of wings fans the air. A group of finches lands on the end of a branch on a nearby piñon. One finch playfully sticks its beak into a snow pillow. Curious and inquisitive, the finches are the first sign of life to come out of hiding. Then, a squawking scrub jay sails in and disrupts the silence. The finches scatter and fly away.

Squawking the whole time, the jay lands with a flourish and bobs its head in quick motions demanding attention. Perhaps it sees itself as the security guard of the wilderness.

Its squawking warns me that it is watching. Like a prodded vagrant, I move along. Snow squeaks under my boots, and off it flies with one last squawk.

Coyote tracks enter from the left farther down the trail. Following the land's natural contour, the tracks disappear to the right, their path more meaningful than the human-made trail I follow.

Around a large prickly pear, the snow has been smudged with dirt scratched by cloven feet, preserving another story. The prints are much smaller than deer tracks. They could only have been left by busy javelina as they rooted for food. I wish I had seen them, their bristly gray coats covered in white and maybe a delicate snowflake clinging to an eyelash.

With a whoosh and a thud, a clump of snow falls off a tree. The sound snaps me out of the fantasy. Clouds dissolve, and the sun begins to melt the snow, exposing dark, wet soil and patches of shiny sandstone. Navajo Indians call such a scene the Blanket of Life. As the snow gradually melts, I am reminded why. Unlike rain, snowmelt moisture is taken gradually into the soil, nourishing the deep roots of desert plants. In time, the plants will bring forth the wild foods of life for the flittering birds, footloose coyotes, and rummaging javelina wandering this land.

Under clouds of a breaking storm, above, the cliffs of Munds Mountain catch late-afternoon light.

The first light of morning, right, highlights a ridge of snow-covered ponderosa pine trees in upper Oak Creek Canyon.

Engorged by runoff water, Oak Creek tumbles through Slide Rock State Park, above, and, right, past Cathedral Rock emerging from storm clouds. Both snowmelt and summer monsoon rains can create a powerful flow in the normally mild-mannered stream.

Big Water

[JOURNAL ENTRY]

March 18

BRIGHT FLASHES, BOOMING thunder, and heavy rain drumming on the roof woke me again last night. Unlike winter's usual gentle rains, these recent El Niño storms resemble summer monsoons. By afternoon, I finally get my work done and drive up Oak Creek Canyon to see what the rains have done to the creek.

Standing alongside the road near Encinoso Picnic Area, people are staring up into the canyon. High above pours Purtymun Falls. The bold, white ribbon shines brightly as sunlight breaks through the clouds. Tucked into a large cove of dark, columnar basalt, the waterfall comes to life only with melting snow or big rain. Today, it once again cascades over the edge of the Colorado Plateau — mesmerizing everyone who sees it.

Driving farther up the canyon, I pass Manzanita Campground on the right, cross the bridge at Slide Rock, then pass Junipine Resort on the left, and finally park along the highway near Bootlegger Campground. I walk down the steep bank to the creek.

Oak Creek is no longer mild-mannered. Its roar signals that it has become a raging, forceful river. Large waves crash wildly and aggressively in the gray-brown water, cloudy with silt, powerfully racing over boulders rather than around them. The current churns strongly straight into the trunks of sycamore trees.

Only days ago, I returned home from three weeks of rafting down the rapids-filled Colorado River in the Grand Canyon. Now, here before me a classic V-shaped tongue leads straight into the center of a rapid. Lateral waves slap hard. Water pours over submerged boulders, leaving holes in the stream. And a large, swirling eddy spins with the release of constricted energy. Today, all the familiar whitewater patterns that river runners know so well transform Oak Creek.

The large, deep roar of Oak Creek scrubs my mind and enlivens my soul. Once again I feel an inner recharge from boldly moving water. I feel an unexpected freedom and begin singing.

As I head back to my van in the twilight, I put my hands in my coat pockets to keep them warm. In one of the pockets I find a piece of hard candy left from when I last wore this coat — on the river trip. I untwist the wrapper and pop the butterscotch into my mouth. Making up the words as I go, I begin the drive down Oak Creek Canyon, singing in the dark: *Moving water, you soothe my restless mind, you bring comfort to my soul . . .*

Ephemeral Beauty

[JOURNAL ENTRY]

March 20

A RAINBOW FLOATS out of the lower waterfall. Soaring high above me, a raven ignores this hidden, secret place. Higher still, in the cream-colored cliffs, another waterfall continuously leaps several hundred feet straight down. Each year — for only a few days — melted snow free-falls off this cliff of Wilson Mountain.

A passing storm covered the cliffs with a foot of snow. But today the air temperature feels more like spring, and the snow is melting fast. The upper waterfall seems to be pouring out of the clear sky. Wind-blown mist sprays sideways, wetting stripes of desert varnish on the cliffs. The long, dark, vertical stripes glisten black as raven feathers.

The rainbow — brilliantly pure and innocent — dances with wispy curtains of mist in the lower waterfall. The radiant colors grow more luminous for a moment, then fade, only to return again and again with their swaying motion.

Meanwhile, the lower fall continues to splash and slap against the rocks with a light, syncopated rhythm. In a series of overlapping, rumbling notes, its ephemeral stream carries the water away to the dark, narrow canyon further down. I try to listen simultaneously to the splashes of water falling and the rustle of the small stream. It seems surprisingly difficult to combine them as the sounds play in my head.

I close my eyes for a moment before starting the hike back down. I want to remember this place. The small and wavering rainbow. The high-soaring raven. The series of waterfalls. And then, with my eyes still closed, I hear the diverse water sounds transform into the sound of little children laughing and playing. ◯

A rainbow, below, arcs across the dark, post-storm sky directly above Snoopy Rock.

Canyon Music

[JOURNAL ENTRY]
May 23

WHEN I WAS last here in West Fork, it was late autumn, and a chill hung in the air. Then, the canyon floor gave off the damp, rich aroma of decomposing leaves, and winter darkness was arriving a little earlier each evening.

Today, I sit under a young alder tree beside the stream on a warm spring day. Wild seeds are sprouting everywhere; and a light, sweet smell of plant juices puts hope in the air. A variety of wildflowers grows among young bracken ferns and purple-blooming lupine. Out of this forest of waist-high ferns, a ponderosa granddaddy towers skyward. A breeze passing through its branches smells faintly of warm vanilla; up high, bright green tips announce new growth.

Water flows over layers of polished stone with flute music seeming to echo softly out of the ripples before coming to rest in quiet pools.

I want to capture it all, somehow; keep it for later. But I know I can't. So before I begin hiking again, I pause to absorb the light, the flow, and the peaceful music of the Earth.

After about 3 miles I enter a long, narrow chamber where the canyon walls enclose the stream. The only route here, I remember, is up the middle of the stream. Just beyond the narrows the stream flows over terraced sandstone that until today has been my farthest turn-around point. It's behind me now, and I continue on.

Farther up, I reach another narrow chamber filled with a long pool with water over my head in places. Along its length stretches a natural shelf about as narrow as my foot is wide and just inches above the water level. I see no other options, just this one route through. Walking my hands against the canyon wall, I begin traversing the shelf. Where it widens I look down into the tranquil water. Looking back at me is the brownish-blue soul of a deep canyon pool.

After a bend, 4 or 5 miles into the canyon, I come to a longer, deeper pool. To go any farther, it seems, will require a cold swim. Searching the canyon walls for an alternative, I notice a faint game trail hidden in the brush on the left bank. The trail leads up and then across a steeply leaning slope. I take it.

Carrying my pack of camera gear across the loose slope, I feel gravity trying to pull me down into the water waiting 30 feet below. It doesn't win — this time. I safely make it to the far end of the pool.

Without a doubt, I have reached a special place. Forming an open-ended chamber, the canyon walls project a gracefulness that appears carved by a giant's knife. Mosses, grasses, and flowers grow from moist cracks. This place just plain feels good, and I settle in to stay for awhile.

A watery orchestra of full-bodied sounds fills the chamber. My attention goes to one tone, follows it awhile, and then moves upstream and down to follow others. A bass note coming from upstream emits a deep, rich quality that reminds me of water being poured into a large, earthen jar.

After I enjoy the music for awhile, a burst of wind comes racing down the canyon and overpowers the water sounds. I look up as it sways the large trees clinging to the canyon walls. Upstream, a thick, silver log above the water is wedged between the walls, seeming to hold them apart. It testifies to the power of raging storm water sometime in the violent past.

After pausing a few moments longer to gather this place into my memory, I hike back downstream to one of the canyon narrows and abruptly stop.

On the smooth canyon wall dances a light show. Twisting reflections broadcast ripples, waves, pulsating with ever-changing patterns, magnified, exhilarating, and bright. The shapes hypnotically change and then the patterns move slower and then slower. My spirit is dazzled.

With my foot I stir the surface of the water, and again the show begins. Music for the eyes performed by sunlight, water, and my passage between canyon walls. My spirit shines brighter as my soul dances with the music of this wild canyon. ◯

Blue-purple lupine flowers, left, surround a cluster of bracken fern on the canyon floor of West Fork.

Right, early morning calm allows a perfect reflection in West Fork Canyon.

Renewal

[JOURNAL ENTRY]
September 15

WHEN I FIRST found this place, it was a mixture of dappled shade, deep water, and natural privacy. Alder trees arched long branches high over Oak Creek, screening the midday sun. Cool water hugged the cliffs and waited for swimmers on the hottest of summer days.

A few years later, floods engorged with El Niño rains tore violently through Oak Creek Canyon. Massive tree trunks, twisted and torn branches, loose rocks, and other debris tumbled downstream, smashing into anything in the way, including the alders. Breaking and uprooting several of the tall trees, the storm-maddened water carried them away and heaved the broken pieces haphazardly into logjams still visible today.

Without the trees, the swimming hole was starkly exposed. The summertime sun now baked the dark basalt boulders on the shoreline. The comfortable shade had disappeared and along with it the feeling of privacy. Only a memory existed of how it was. I didn't return for several years.

Today, a healthy, young alder thicket once again hides the swimming hole. The young trees aren't nearly as tall as their predecessors, but they are returning some of the magic to the place.

Standing on a boulder on the shoreline, I look over my secret retreat. Downstream, shimmering reflections mix a palette of back-lighted greens. Upstream, a small waterfall rushes over rocks in shades of dark turquoise, gray, and white. Before me the depth of the pool shows through the surface. I step out of my river sandals and take a deep breath.

Headfirst with arms extended, I am flying over the water. Time's passage slows. First my fingertips, next my arms, now my head, torso, legs, and feet enter the underwater world of ochre-colored highlights and blue-gray shadows. I silently glide through the deep, cool water.

Time's normal cadence resumes as I surface. I shake water from my hair, and the current moves me downstream slowly. I swim farther downstream toward a huge boulder, circle behind it and come to rest in a gentle eddy. Steamboat Rock and Shiprock loom in the western sky. The distant rock formations fit seamlessly with the nearby cliff rising from the edge of the pool. This part of the canyon feels deep and secluded.

I swim from behind the boulder, and the gentle current pushes against my body. I swim upstream, staying near the cliff wall to avoid the main current. Farther upstream, approaching the waterfall, I begin to swim more strongly through the boiling water and reach the side of the falls.

In the foaming water directly below the falls, I see a tumbled stack of boulders and cobbles. My hands search underwater and find a grip. Hanging on, I pull my body into the falls and turn backwards; the water cascades loudly onto my neck and shoulders. The constant roar consumes my world. I can barely hear my thoughts as I slide farther into the falls, brace myself, and receive the full power of the rushing water. I push my feet against boulders and press back into the falls. Deep vibrations shake and invigorate my body. Water shoots out over each shoulder in clear sheets. I struggle to hold my position.

Satisfied, I release my perch, and the current quickly pushes me into the pool below. I swim to a sun-filled eddy and float in the calm stillness. Cliffs, trees, and the infinite sky rise overhead. My body hangs almost weightless, slightly rising and sinking with each breath.

Relaxed, I draw a deep breath and swim underwater toward shore. Climbing onto shoreline boulders, my bare feet feel the warmth radiating from them, yet goose bumps pattern my arms. Bright, clear water droplets cling to my skin. They flash tiny rainbow sparks. In the warmth of the sun I begin to absorb the wider spectrum of sights and sounds that are sharing this place.

I feel alive. I am not scattered in emotional disharmony. I am whole again. My mind and body and spirit revel in the healing power of being with the water. This is the essence of enjoying summer, and I feel refreshed to the core. ◯

In a quiet section of upper Oak Creek Canyon, a canopy of streamside trees creates dappled light and shade on mounds of watercress.

Gibraltar, a formation on the west ridge of Lee Mountain, takes on different looks as it responds to sunlight and fog, above, and to sunlight filtering through the clouds, opposite top.

Morning frost clings to oak leaves, opposite bottom, in the shade of Boynton Canyon.

At sunset, following panel [pages 62 and 63], Chimney Rock casts its shadow on a ridge of Capitol Butte, while a nearly full moon rises above Coffeepot Rock and Ship Rock.

In the Midst of Something Rare

[JOURNAL ENTRY]

December 29

TINY MANZANITA AND scrub-oak leaves are jeweled with rain droplets. Fog roams the valley. A moist, cool wind blows as I find my way to the top of a knoll. Veils of fog magically become clouds and turn again into wispy fog.

I discover deer tracks in a ravine forested with Arizona cypress leading toward the higher knoll. I follow them in the soft, wet soil, trying not to leave my own tracks as I step from rock to rock. Near the top, the damp ground turns to solid sandstone — and the tracks disappear. High above, the cliff face of Gibraltar also disappears.

Gibraltar, 800 feet of solid stone, closely resembles the famous landmark off Spain. The square-cornered fortress begins a series of cliffs rolling southward. Paralleling it on the opposite side of the valley is another series of cliffs called The Transept. Piñon, juniper, and Arizona cypress trees pepper the open valley between the two ridges. Suspended moisture hangs low and mysterious over the top of stately Courthouse Butte rising 1,200 feet above the floor of the valley to the south.

Long ago John Muir wrote: "When the storm began . . . I lost no time in pushing out into the woods to enjoy it. For on such occasions Nature has always something rare to show us . . . "

His words rang in my head as I began this hike. I knew full well that another rainstorm was close at hand. I wanted to be out in the storm. I wanted to feel and experience something rare.

Fog near Bell Rock transforms again and now seems to be streaming in long waves. It pushes forward and then recedes. It curls under and floats upward, hesitates, and then blows free.

In the next moment, two graceful arms of fog reach around Courthouse as a silky cascade begins dancing over the top. The face of Courthouse fades and disappears as the sensual mists flow across the talus slopes and down onto the valley floor.

The fog transforms into a dancing chorus line, traveling forward, moving energetically up the valley's contours. With its flowing veils sweeping over trees, the fog moves halfway

up into the layered sandstone cliffs. Losing their color, and then their details, the cliffs disappear into various shades of ghostly gray.

The storm moves quickly. It melts everything in its path into elemental shapes.

Soon, the nearby trees fade into the gray. Then, mysteriously, the sun-splashed top of Gibraltar emerges out of the mists. But only moments pass before it is gone again. The clouds and fog settle in to stay.

Gentle rain begins coming down, tapping the hood of my rain jacket with soft staccato rhythms. In the increasing grayness I walk back down the knoll, retracing the deer path I had taken. The path descends into the ravine, and I re-enter the grove of wet Arizona cypress trees just as the fog brightens.

The trees — isolated within the white fog — look like dancers impersonating trees. They are graceful and serene, with rain-darkened branches reaching upward in flowing lines. The bluish-green color of their fragrant needles comes alive against the light backdrop of fog. They seem filled with invisible, sparkling energy.

These trees love this cool, wet weather. In this land of cactus and lizards, they are survivors of the last Ice Age. Like their ancient ancestors who greeted this land's first human inhabitants, they help make the air we breathe.

I take a slow, deep breath — a fresh-mint sensation fills my lungs. I realize I am in the midst of something rare. I feel satisfied. As I walk away, a soft applause of raindrops follows me. ◌

Chapter 4

The Living Earth

There is nothing inorganic. The earth is not a mere fragment of dead history . . . but living poetry . . . Not a fossil earth, but a living earth.

— Henry David Thoreau, *Walden*

THE LANDS WE KNOW AS Sedona hold stories of tropical oceans, stories of volcanoes, and stories of drifting continents. These stories are told on a stage so large, about a time frame so enormous, that we hardly can comprehend their magnitude. Yet, hidden in the canyons and mesas are smaller stories that tell of mystery and grace and beauty where arches mystify gravity, massive stones balance on one another, and spires soar skyward.

Sedona's geologic monuments were carved by natural forces from the very edge of the mighty Colorado Plateau. The plateau covers 130,000 square miles — spreading from Arizona north and east into Utah, Colorado, and New Mexico — an area almost three times the size of New York state.

From almost any point in the Sedona area, you can see the multi-hued horizontal layers of the Colorado Plateau laid down eons ago; river silts and shallow tidal flats; sand

From a sandstone shelf eroded into Munds Mountain, left, the westward view reveals Twin Buttes and the Nuns (left of center). Munds Mountain defines the southern edge of the 130,000-square mile Colorado Plateau and makes up the dramatic backdrop for much of Sedona.

Natural arches are scattered throughout Sedona's topography. The more popular ones are Window Rock, right, hidden near Slide Rock, as well as Devil's Bridge on the north side of Capitol Butte, Vultee Arch in Sterling Canyon, and Fay Canyon Arch.

A female collared lizard, above, basks in the sun along the Cow Pies Trail, which can be reached via Schnebly Hill Road.

dunes; and marine sediments, fossils, and lava solidified into stone.

A dozen tectonic plates float on Earth's partly molten mantle. The plates have moved slowly like nomadic tribes. The land we know as Arizona rides with the North American Plate. Over a vast period, it has migrated from south of the Equator into the Northern Hemisphere. The plate still is moving one-half to 1 inch per year or about 50 miles every 6 million years.

During this migration, several events have altered Earth. One of the most drastic occurred 65 million years ago after a mountain-sized asteroid crashed off Mexico's Yucatan Peninsula. Scientists believe the devastation caused by the asteroid may have been 100 times greater than the impact that caused Meteor Crater just 40 miles east of Flagstaff.

Airborne debris from the Yucatan asteroid blocked the sun's warmth for years. Without sunlight, green plants withered. As food sources from plants disappeared, other forms of life starved as well. More than 75 percent of life on the planet became extinct — most famous, of course, being the dinosaurs — during this one event. As the North American Plate drifted with the land that would become Sedona, the Earth experi-

enced five completely separate periods of global extinction.

The North American Plate also experienced a series of ice ages, uplifts, and endless erosion. Out of this constant change has come the beauty of Sedona's landscape.

AS YOU HIKE up Cathedral Rock Trail, you literally are walking over the past — the durable remains of what existed before. As you climb, your boots are making contact with stone formed 275 million years ago. At that time, you would have been walking along a beach of warm ocean waves. Strong winds coming across gigantic reddish-orange coastal dunes would have blown sand in your eyes. Blowing down from the north, the sand mixed in the tidal areas day after day, month after month, for 5 million years. Immense overlaying pressure and time consolidated a 700-foot-thick sandstone layer. Geologists call this the Schnebly Hill Formation.

Sedona and Grand Canyon, both cut from the Colorado Plateau, share the same geology, except for the Schnebly Hill Formation. Its distinctly orange sandstone forms most of the well-known rock formations in Sedona, including Bell Rock, Courthouse Butte, Coffeepot Rock, and Cathedral Rock.

Clockwise from below left: Sunset glows on Teapot Rock, morning fog shrouds Coffeepot Rock, and sunrise strikes Bell Rock. Opposite, sunshine spotlights details of the spires on Cathedral Rock, including the Mace at far right.

Below the Schnebly Hill Formation you will see masses of dark, reddish-brown rock that often form slopes. This layer was created from sediment washing off the Ancestral Rocky Mountains. Rivers carried the silt into floodplains and mudflats for 10 million years. Eventually it formed into 300-foot-deep shale called the Hermit Formation.

Below the Hermit shale is the Supai Group layer of rock. Going back another 35 million years, we see a shallow sea. The sea withdrew and returned several times while mixing with silt and sand brought in by rivers. Swamps and deltas formed into a layer 200 to 500 feet thick. The Supai Group layer is the bedrock on which Sedona is built.

Hidden below the Supai Group, Redwall limestone forms the spectacular cliffs in Grand Canyon but in Sedona only shows itself near lower Dry Creek and the mouth of Sycamore Canyon. Redwall serves an important function — storing water in its vast underground caverns. Although very strong, limestone dissolves when in constant contact with water. Rain and snowmelt percolate down until the gravity-drawn flow is stopped by the hard layer below the Redwall limestone. The trapped water eats away at the limestone and creates huge caverns hundreds of feet below the surface. Cavern ceilings occasionally collapse. The Devil's Kitchen sinkhole in Soldiers Pass, for example, ruptured the surface in the late 1800s and still erodes.

Look up at the tall spires of Cathedral Rock. From below, you probably can't see the rhythmical breaks in the sandstone that helped create the rock's spires. But from the elevated view of a soaring hawk, you could look down at the sandstone as it spreads out from the spires. The formation looks like loaves of sliced bread. The basin and range topography that extends southward from the Colorado Plateau has been stretched, fracturing into these vertical slices or joints.

The joints invite moisture to hide from the sun. Come winter, cold temperatures energize the powerful force of ice being formed. As ice expands it cracks the rock deeper. Soon, gravity, snowmelt,

Below, hiking guide Dennis Andres (left) and photographer Larry Lindahl enjoy the beauty of Boynton Canyon.

A placid reflection in Pump House Wash, opposite, barely hints at the rushing snowmelt and seasonal rains that powerfully scoured this narrow passageway through the Coconino sandstone.

and rainwater work together to flush out particles loosened in the gap. In spring, in the newly widened space, a seed may land, sprout, and send roots for the moisture stored in the gap. Over years, the roots dig deeper, trapping more water. Winter ice may again expand in the crack. Stone particles again are washed out of the crack and carried into a stream, then a river, and maybe someday the ocean, where they will settle to form yet another geologic layer eons in the future.

Stone exposed to weather is eroding constantly in different ways and rates. Some strata, such as Hermit shale slopes, melt a little under each rainstorm. Limestone cliffs, instead, break off in huge chunks onto the slopes below. Basalt, the hardest of all the local stone, fills the streambed of Oak Creek with gray boulders and cobbles — it is the last to wear down.

HIKING ONE DAY in the side canyon of Oak Creek called Pump House Wash, I came upon a pattern in the streambed sand. Dry riverbeds and washes naturally contain evidence of what lies above. Here, sand had sorted itself into long, separate ribbons colored dark gray and cream. The cream-colored sand was quartz that had eroded down from the Coconino sandstone cliffs stacked above the rust-colored Schnebly Hill Formation. The dark sand was pulverized basalt from ancient lava flows found at even higher elevations. As snowmelt carried sediment from the high country down the wash, the lighter quartz granules washed high up on the shoreline. The heavier basalt sand settled out below, creating the ribbon shapes.

Coconino sandstone, the source material for the light-colored sand, was created during a 5-million-year period when the Sedona region was a parched desert. Sand dunes moved with the wind and covered the region. Driving north past West Fork on State Route 89A, you begin to see the intricate wind patterns in the 500-foot-thick Coconino sandstone layer. The ancient dunes piled up, avalanched down, and piled up even higher. Erosion cutting away the cliffs has revealed the patterns — cross-bedded stripes, slumping angles, and wind swirls — locked in the stone.

When the Sedona region was yet again under seawater, marine sediments sank to the ocean floor, compacting into the 300-foot thick Toroweap Formation. The Toroweap, formed for the next 3 million years after the Coconino sandstone, is a mix of siltstone and gypsum near Sycamore Canyon and sandstone near Sedona. Look for a band of vegetation growing across the cream-colored cliffs between the Toroweap and Coconino layers. Water seeps out here, making a moist environment.

A different type of marine sediment deposited the 350-foot Kaibab limestone layer over the Toroweap. The skeletons of primitive sponges, crinoid stems, seashells, and other sea life, over a 5-million-year span, became the limestone that makes up the rim of Grand Canyon and caps Munds and Lee mountains in Sedona.

The most recent layer was laid on the land 13-15 million years ago when lava oozed from fissures in the Sedona region. The layer forms the gray columnar rock most often seen above the cliffs of light-colored sandstone. A good example

is on Wilson Mountain. Cliffs of basalt, some nearly 500 feet thick, also define the Mogollon Rim, the southern edge of the Colorado Plateau.

In 1923, Zane Grey wrote *The Call of the Canyon,* a story set in West Fork. Describing the canyon's visual appeal on the novel's heroine, Carley, whose roots were in Eastern high society, Grey wrote:

"It fascinated her. There were inaccessible ledges that haunted her with their remote fastnesses. How wonderful would it be to get there, rest there, if that were possible! But only eagles could reach them. There were places, then, that the desecrating hands of man could not touch. The dark caves were mystically potent in their vacant staring out at the world beneath them. The crumbling crags, the toppling ledges, the leaning rocks all threatened to come thundering down at the breath of wind. How deep and soft the red color in contrast with the green! How splendid the sheer bold uplift of gigantic steps!"

The land is always waiting to tell you its ever-changing story. Here in Sedona's red rocks, you will find yourself, much like Carley, "marveling at the forces that had so rudely, violently, and grandly left this monument to nature."

A Place in Between

[JOURNAL ENTRY]
April 4

UP ON STEAMBOAT ROCK, a warm wind tosses my hair when just yesterday fog and snow flirted here all day. They left together during the night, and today there's not a cloud in the sky. The undecided weather says it's springtime, again.

Walking across Steamboat's narrow sandstone deck, I step over remnants of stone walls constructed centuries ago. This vantage point would have been useful; the view spreads in all directions. Below endless open space, Bell Rock appears small out in the distance. You can see a long ways.

Woven across the land is an abstract pattern of piñon, juniper, and cypress trees. Due east — directly opposite the sun — the trees have no visible shadow and the vegetation looks like pale blue-green velvet draping Casner Canyon.

After traversing the length of the sandstone deck, I stop at the southwest end. The sun is painting afternoon shadows among Munds Mountain's white cliffs, in between the rich-orange towers of Mitten Ridge, and down into Oak Creek Canyon. The beautifully eroded ridge of sandstone formations divides green hills from rich blue sky.

To the west, silver strands shimmer far below in the darkness of a small canyon. The sun-reflecting runoff is the only sign of yesterday's fog and snow. Higher in Soldiers Pass, the Sphinx and Mitten cast strange, horizontal blue-gray shadow beams that float weightless above the ground. Capitol Butte rises tall in the sky.

Kneeling down with my eyes close to the sandstone, I cautiously crawl forward. Gripping the edge, I hang my head over. The cliff

drops away — 200 feet straight down. I look down the length of it. Stripes trace the curving contours of the rock I am lying on. A glossy black raven flashes below. Its shadow races to keep up, flying wingtip to wingtip across the cliff face.

I carefully pull back and sit up. A bird whistles a sweet hello. A red and brown finch sits atop a stunted cliffrose. The male house finch is not completely red like the striking male cardinal nor plain brown like a common sparrow. He is a color in between. He whistles again, and I look over to him. I'm too close for his comfort. He flies a few more feet away, landing on top of a juniper.

Again he whistles hello. His voice is so pure. Inspired by the greeting, I whistle back. He looks at me, perhaps wondering what I mean. But he whistles again, anyway. I wait a moment and whistle back. We carry on, falling into a rhythm — his turn, my turn, his turn, my turn.

Then he ups the ante and shifts from his plain hello whistle to a much more difficult song, trilling two distinct tones at the same time. I cannot play back this song. Instead, I take my turn by making up a more complex reply. Looking me in the eye, he cocks his head. Again he replies, making a beautiful series of trilling combinations.

When he is finished, I begin my reply and whistle somewhat longer than before. The finch starts in, and we are now a duet — bird and human. Harmonizing with such a beautiful singer, feeling the connection of sharing music, I smile as he looks at me. Then he flies off the treetop, straight down, over the cliff edge. I cannot follow. ◌

A bridled titmouse, above, pauses on a sycamore tree branch along Oak Creek. Its song is a repeated two-syllable phrase, similar to a chickadee's.

Spires above Long Canyon, right, frame a cluster of rock formations crowned by Capitol Butte.

Turning Around

[JOURNAL ENTRY]

June 21

PERCHED ON A weathered sandstone bluff flowing out from Chimney Rock, I look into the setting sun's glow. How do I describe this sunset? Luminous . . . primordial . . . transcendent . . . elemental . . . glorious . . . They all fall short. The color defies description.

With words set aside, I envision Georgia O'Keefe painting her feeling of sky and Earth, a feeling of being connected with the whirlwind cosmos. And now, in an age-old ritual, I watch the sun coming home to Bear Mountain. First they kiss, then embrace. Finally with the workday done, the bright orb slides out of sight behind the massive horizon.

Turning away, I look east toward the distant shadowed valley where Courthouse Butte rises up, a crimson block of shining hot metal. The red light waves are strong, determined, and energetic. They are still piercing the curved edge of the atmosphere while all the other colors are getting bounced into space.

The Earth gradually rotates Sedona away from the sun, and Courthouse turns deeper and deeper red. Only Wilson, Munds, and Lee mountains stand tall enough now to receive the last of the light. But finally, with the fire extinguished, shadows and highlights blend into one. Reflected light lingers, making the cliffs appear to softly glow from within.

Today the sun reaches a solstice and celebrates the first day of summer. The days will lengthen no longer. For the next six months, each day gets just a little shorter.

Into the changing hues of infinite space, two ravens fly with their feet tucked into little fists and their long black feathers fingering the glowing air. They chortle and caw back and forth. I am a stranger to the meaning but not to the melody as their voices echo among the chambers of the bluff. First one, and then the other, bounce-lands and hops sideways, finding a place on the rounded ledge. As a golden sheen flashes off their black feathers, I wish I too could be a raven, sharing the privilege of flight, just for a little while.

Instead, I walk back along the edge of the bluff. I spot a silhouetted pair of agave stalks pointing ahead. The twins, growing only a few feet apart, stand ready with bright yellow flower buds offering sweetness to insects and hummingbirds and the heavens. The agave plants mark my route down.

While enough light lingers to show me the way, I carefully descend the crack in the cliff. Halfway down I come upon a cliffrose hiding a few fresh blossoms among its flowers already gone to seed. I lean over the feathery seed pods to sniff a fresh flower. I slowly inhale, and into my head flows a fragrance as delicate as the glowing twilight. The scent mixes hints of beeswax and warm butterscotch pudding into a moment of simple ecstasy. I hesitate within the moment and resume climbing down, carrying the delicious, glowing memory. After all, this is only the first day of summer. ◝

Golden hues paint Capitol Butte and the rock formations of Mitten Ridge on Schnebly Hill during the last moments of a summer sunset.

Curiosity

[JOURNAL ENTRY]

November 17

CLIMBING OFF-TRAIL, I have used up more than an hour. I stumble around a landmine of agave. The plant's spikes reach out to stab my shins. After escaping the agave and traversing a long, steep slope of manzanita, I find a thicket of scrub oak barricading my way. Each tiny oak leaf is edged in stickers. Then I find my way right into a bunch of downed piñon trees with curled branches lying in a mess across the slope.

I stop to catch my breath in all this struggle to find a particularly well-hidden place that has intrigued me for months. My first sight of it was last spring when a climbing partner, Bronze Black, and I had bushwhacked to get up to a lookout. On top of the unnamed point we nicknamed it "Pinnacle Peak."

After taking in the panorama, we looked down over the eastern side, straight down — nearly 1,200 feet. At the bottom we saw a space, closed in by folded sandstone, too mysterious to ignore. With a small point-and-shoot camera, I made a quick record of it.

So, here I am — searching. Still breathing hard, I drop my daypack. It's been warmer than usual, and my back is soaked in

An agave, left, matures with an expanding rosette of spiked leaves, perhaps years away from sending up a flower stalk.

sweat. I pull out one of my water bottles and look around. As my heavy breathing begins to subside, silence fills the space around me. Not a lonely, empty silence. Instead, it's restorative and comforting — the soothing sound of solitude.

Before starting out again, I try to chart a route to the secret place. I look into the snapshot and compare it one last time with the topography of the cliffs. That's when I notice a cavern maybe 100 feet above me. What might this out-of-the-way cave be hiding? I can't resist the urge to explore the cave.

The approach goes up a loose, steep-angled, dirt slope. With each step I slide back a little but eventually reach a ledge that starts less than 2 feet wide and narrows. Knowing better, I start out on the thin strip of stone with focused steps. After covering about 30 or 40 feet, I come to a sandstone rubble pile. I sidestep over it and go another 10 feet. The path now is only a little wider than the length of my boots.

The cave's dark opening beckons. I look forward at the last few steps necessary to get there. Then my gaze falls over the edge. Down. Way down. The distance unsettles me. I sink into the ledge and hug the wall as my legs wobble. Looking straight ahead, I force myself to breathe away the vertigo.

The cavern calls again, "You've gotten this far. Why not try?"

I ponder my bravado. What if there is nothing inside the cave? Nothing but the packrat's collection I think I can already see. I look at the last few steps necessary to get across the ledge. I stare at the cavern. Once again I look over the edge into a 50- or 60-foot drop. The feeling in my stomach says, "No way!"

Reluctantly I turn back, sidestepping across the cliff face toward safety. With a feeling of relief, I reach the rubble pile and pause to look back at the cavern. A rustling sound begins. It sounds like hard, dry leaves blowing across sandstone. Still not understanding, I listen more closely. The sound increases in tempo. Now it's unmistakable — there is a rattlesnake on this ledge!

I freeze. Terrified. Somewhere in the rock pile near my feet, the venomous pit viper buzzes even louder. My legs tremble. I wish I

were anywhere but here.

The snake remains hidden. I picture it striking me in a lightning-fast thrust. If its needle-sharp fangs penetrate my leg, I will feel a stabbing, hot pain. I fear what my reaction might be. Below me looms the height of a fatal drop.

Knowing that nausea, swelling, and shock soon follow snakebite, I imagine my need for emergency medical care. The enzymes in the toxic venom would attack and quickly begin dissolving my muscle or nerve tissue, depending on what type of rattlesnake it is. If it's a Mojave green, the venom could disable my respiratory system. I fully absorb the severity of my situation.

I still cannot see the buzzing snake. What should I do? The terror exceeds any I have known. I feel cold. Attempts to breathe are awkward. I must do something. I can't stand here forever. I search. There are not enough handholds or footholds for me to go up or down the cliff face. I can't reach anything to defend myself against the snake. There is really no choice. I must step over the rattlesnake. Period.

My legs increasingly wobble. I can't stand the anxiety anymore. So I risk everything in a huge gamble. Ever so slowly, I lift my front foot.

I fully expect to see the rattler's wide-open jaws come flying out of the rock pile. Straight into my left ankle — just above the foot that is now supporting all my weight. What if I don't move slowly enough? Or steadily enough? And after I am bitten, will I be able to bushwhack back to my van? Will there be enough time to get to help?

I lift my right foot higher.

Concentrate. Use all the self-control you can muster. Keep the leg up high.

I move it inch by inch over the rock pile. I bring it down so slowly it seems to take forever. The foot makes it to the other side.

Then I wait. I stand straddling the rock pile.

Can I finish what I have started? When will the impact of the snakebite happen? I know I need to continue.

I begin to lift my left foot.

The buzzing suddenly flares louder. My leg feels so heavy. It takes all my strength

Scattered clouds cast a pattern of light and shadow, opposite, into Boynton Canyon. The view is from the soaring cliffs along the northeastern summit of Bear Mountain.

to lift it higher. I coax it to move over the spine-chilling sound. I see a foot in mid-air. It belongs to someone else. I can't really be doing this.

As slowly as I can, I set the foot down beside my other foot. I don't look down. The yawning space still pulls at my back. My heart is pumping ice water. I feel light-headed. Dizzy. Sick to my stomach. I force myself to take one more very slow sidestep. Then, nothing.

Faintly, then louder, through fuzzy, scrambled static I hear myself. *You have made it past the rattlesnake. You have not been bitten. You are now out of danger.* Slowly, I comprehend. Now it's real time again.

Watching the rock pile I want to look the snake in the eye. My primal self wants to kill it. Punish it for my fear. Come out, you coward. I am ready. He doesn't show. Exhausted, I move farther and farther away.

Out of the fear comes a realization. I am only a guest, here, in this wild place. The rattlesnake only wants to survive — live one more day. It was its own life it was protecting. But without a doubt, he has triggered a most basic emotion — primal fear. Fear of death. Existence terminated. Game over.

This unexpected encounter has distracted both snake and human. Soon, a packrat or some other animal will — once again — be the snake's desired quarry. The snake remains hidden within the pile of sandstone. I leave it to its age-old challenge of survival.

I shoulder my pack and carry on. As I head around the next corner I look back, one last time, at the cavern. Still searching for that secret place in the snapshot, I realize the limitations of my photo map. Or any map, for that matter. It can show you how to get somewhere, but it can't tell you what's going to happen once you are there. ◠

Red Rock Country

Whether you like rugged mountaintop vistas or gentle creekside strolls, there is a hike just for you.

HIKING IN RED ROCK COUNTRY of Sedona infuses one's soul with memories to treasure for a lifetime. So, bring your camera and also consider bringing a small journal, and a watercolor set or a sketch pad. Let this unique landscape speak to you.

In the heat of summer you will need a quart of water for each hour, a wide-brim hat, sunscreen, sunglasses, and light-colored clothing.

In late fall, winter, and early spring, prepare for occasional strong winds and variable temperatures with wind-proof clothing, rain protection, lightweight gloves, and a warm hat.

Always bring a flashlight or headlamp and a few extra snacks just in case your hike extends beyond sunset. Take your cell phone, but be aware that reception is very limited in canyon areas. Additional gear for longer hikes should include a map, compass, first aid kit, and lighter or matches.

A bit of caution includes protecting the fragile desert environment and artifacts of those who lived here hundreds of years ago. Avoid damaging the black-crusted soil along trails, as this living cryptobiotic skin takes decades to form and transform sand into living soil for plants. Leave ancient artifacts where you find them for others to enjoy.

Parking at trailheads and along all Coconino National Forest Service roads in Red Rock Country requires a Red Rock Pass. Detailed information on purchasing passes, as well as recreational topics, is available online at www.redrockcountry.org or by calling (928) 282-4119 or (928) 203-7500.

❿ Corresponds to trailheads located on the map.

Easy *Hikes*

⓯ RED ROCK CROSSING AT CRESCENT MOON PICNIC AREA

A gentle stroll along Oak Creek provides photographers with the classic sunset shot of Cathedral Rock reflected in a natural pool rimmed by red sandstone. Paved trails from the parking lot lead to dirt paths meandering a mile upstream to swim areas.

Drive west from West Sedona toward Cottonwood on 89A, turn left at the stoplight near Sedona High School onto Upper Red Rock Loop Road, follow it 1.8 miles, turn left onto Chavez Ranch Road, cross the bridge, continue as road bends to right, and enter Crescent Moon picnic area with the gate on left. Day-use fee required.

⓲ BELL ROCK NEAR VILLAGE OF OAK CREEK

Easy access leads directly onto sandstone shelves, up sinuous gullies, and over weather-rounded mounds. Views along the 2-mile roundtrip include Courthouse Butte, Munds and Lee mountains with Twin Buttes and Cathedral Rock in the distance.

Drive along State 179 to the north end of the Village of Oak Creek, turn into the Bell Rock Pathway Vista parking lot. Follow the trail sign to the Bell Rock Pathway which skirts Bell Rock until the sandstone trail is marked with 2-foot tall rock cairns.

⓾ SEVEN SACRED POOLS IN SOLDIER PASS

A moderate up-and-down trail leads through an enchanted forest to a dramatic sink hole in a quarter-mile and to a series of small pools after a half-mile. The pools provide water for wildlife below a view of Coffee Pot Rock and Capitol Butte.

Between Uptown Sedona and West Sedona, turn north at the stoplight onto Soldier Pass Road, go 2.7 miles, turn right onto Rim Shadows Drive, continue one-third mile to gated entrance road on left, and park at the end. Read posted schedule of the overnight gate closure.

⓬ WILSON CANYON FROM MIDGLEY BRIDGE

A gentle 1.5-mile trail meanders into a scented forest of Arizona cypress nestled below red rock cliffs and towering 7,122-foot Wilson Mountain. Grizzly bears no longer exist in Arizona, but pioneer Richard Wilson was killed in this canyon by a wounded grizzly in 1885.

Drive north from Uptown Sedona 1 mile up Oak Creek Canyon on 89A, cross over Midgley Bridge, and immediately park on left. The trail begins on the far end of the vista parking area.

Hikes along Creeks

⓭ ALLEN'S BEND ALONG OAK CREEK AT GRASSHOPPER POINT

Ambling through Oak Creek Canyon, this half-mile trail leads to the creekside, on the right, after crossing over small boulders and cobbles. An ideal hike to experience the rustle of flowing water under a canopy of tall trees.

Drive from Uptown Sedona 2.5 miles up Oak Creek Canyon on 89A to the Grasshopper Point Recreation Area on the right and follow the road to the bottom parking lot with bathrooms. Day-use fee required.

❶ WEST FORK IN UPPER OAK CREEK CANYON

The 3-mile trail winds through a wooded canyon with several stepping-stone crossings of a clear running stream that echoes softly beneath enormous cliffs. Small groves of bigtooth maple trees turn brilliant red, orange, and yellow in late autumn.

Drive from Uptown Sedona 10.5 miles up Oak Creek Canyon on 89A, and carefully turn left into the gated entrance at a sharp curve. Day-use fee required.

⓳ SYCAMORE CREEK CANYON NEAR COTTONWOOD

Access to this riparian canyon requires almost an hour of driving, but the mellow atmosphere and lack of people may appeal to hardy hikers wanting peace of mind. The 4-mile trail sharply descends to the shady canyon floor and then follows the flowing creek upstream.

Drive on 89A through West Sedona, continue 20 miles to Cottonwood, take Main Street, then Broadway out of town to Tuzigoot National Monument road on right, cross the bridge, turn left on first dirt road, and follow Forest Service Road 131 for 11 miles to parking area.

Hikes to Natural Arches

❾ DEVIL'S BRIDGE IN DRY CREEK BASIN

The steep 1-mile trail stairsteps up to the tall sandstone arch. Expansive views from the arch on the east side of Capitol Butte include Secret Mountain, Dry Creek Basin, and the Mogollon Rim.

Drive to West Sedona, turn north at the stoplight onto Dry Creek Road, after 2 miles turn right onto the rough dirt of Forest Service Road 152 (also called Vultee Arch Road), and park on the right after 1.5 miles.

❷ VULTEE ARCH IN STERLING CANYON

A sturdy sandstone arch spanning a 40-foot ravine awaits hikers 1.5 miles into Sterling Canyon. The easy trail meanders along a shaded sandy wash gently climbing through a forested canyon (thankfully spared during the catastrophic 2006 wildfire). A signed spur trail to the left ends at a smooth stone terrace below the arch.

Drive to West Sedona, turn north at the stoplight onto Dry Creek Road, after 2 miles turn right onto the rough, dirt road, FR 152 (Vultee Arch Road), and park at the end after 4.5 miles.

❺ FAY CANYON ARCH

As a side trip, finding this camouflaged arch is half the fun, before hiking deeper into this scenic, mile-long canyon. Look for a side trail to the right after a half-mile, and climb toward the buff-colored cliffs where a small Indian ruin sits at the base of the arch. The arch looks like an ordinary rock overhang and is hard to spot. Watch the rock wall to the north (right) side of the trail and you'll spot it.

In West Sedona, turn north at the stoplight onto Dry Creek Road, after 3 miles turn left at the Long Canyon Road intersection onto Forest Service Road 152C, after 1.5 miles turn left at Boynton Canyon Road intersection, continue on the paved road a half-mile, and park in the blacktop lot on the left.

Day hikers take a break in a secluded area along the West Fork of Oak Creek Canyon. See "Hikes Along Creeks" on Page 77.

Hikes into Canyons

❻ BOYNTON CANYON

After traversing for a mile around Enchantment Resort, the trail enters the most magical of all the red rock canyons. Near the start look for Kachina Woman spire up the Vista Trail, and then spot ancient ruins in the cliff shadows while hiking the 6.5-mile roundtrip trail. Allow at least three hours to hike to the end and back.

Drive to West Sedona, turn right at the stoplight onto Dry Creek Road, after 3 miles turn left at the Long Canyon Road intersection onto FR 152C, after 1.5 miles turn right at the Boynton Canyon Road intersection, and in a few hundred yards park on the right in the paved lot with rest rooms.

❽ LONG CANYON

After walking around the Seven Canyons golf course, you will begin hiking amongst elegantly tall oak trees and thick stands of Arizona cypress and alligator-bark junipers. Peek-a-boo views along this thickly forested 3-mile trail include shear white crags on Maroon Mountain as it soars above red rock spires and cliffs.

Drive to West Sedona, turn north at the stoplight onto Dry Creek Road, after 3 miles turn right at the intersection onto the Long Canyon Road, and park after a half-mile on the left.

❸ SECRET CANYON

After driving a rough, dirt road through Dry Creek Basin, you reach this vigorous 5-mile trail, which winds into some of the most beautiful back country around Sedona. After crossing the boulder-strewn creekbed, the trail slowly climbs 600 feet into the wide and scenic canyon surrounded by red rocks. After several miles, look in the nearby cliff, on the right, for an arch opening to the sky high above the pines.

Drive to West Sedona, turn right at the stoplight onto Dry Creek Road, after 2 miles turn right onto the rough dirt of FR 152 (Vultee Arch Road), and after 3.5 miles parking is on the left.

Vista *Hikes*

⓰ CATHEDRAL ROCK FROM BACK O' BEYOND ROAD

Climbing solid rock to the saddle of Sedona's most famous formation is ultimately challenging, yet extremely rewarding. Strenuous effort up the three-quarter-mile trail, which seems much longer, leads to stunning red rock views in all directions. Not recommended for those lacking coordination or with a fear of heights.

Drive from Uptown Sedona south on State 179 toward the Village of Oak Creek, after 3.4 miles turn right onto the Back O' Beyond Road, and after a half-mile, park on the left.

⓱ LITTLE HORSE TRAIL TO CHICKEN POINT FROM BELL ROCK PATHWAY

If you don't mind the offbeat names or sharing the vista point with groups on Jeep tours, this little-known trail quickly leaves the highway while gently climbing 300 feet over 3.5 miles to a great view. The seemingly secluded trail reveals Cathedral Rock, Bell Rock, Courthouse Butte, and Gibraltar, as it winds its way up to Chicken Point beside the Nuns and Twin Buttes.

Drive from Uptown Sedona south on 179 toward the Village of Oak Creek, after 3.6 miles turn left into Bell Rock Pathway parking area. Follow the Bell Rock Pathway east for a short ways until a sign at a large wash points left to the Little Horse Trail.

⓫ BRINS MESA FROM JORDAN ROAD IN UPTOWN SEDONA

A moderately strenuous workout combines climbing 600 feet over 2.7 miles to the edge of a sloping mesa with expansive views. Recognizable rock formations beyond a valley of stunted trees include Wilson Mountain, Shiprock, Teapot, Giants Thumb, and the white cliffs of distant Munds Mountain.

Drive north through Uptown Sedona on Jordan Road as it parallels 89A, cross a small bridge after three quarters of a mile and turn left at the end of the road onto West Park Ridge Road. After a half-mile take the dirt road at the end of the cul-de-sac, and in a half-mile park in the large gravel lot.

⓮ MUNDS WAGON TRAIL FROM SCHNEBLY HILL ROAD

The 4-mile, 1,000-foot climb up Bear Wallow Canyon to the Merry-go-round vista point presents long western views of Munds Mountain, Capitol Butte, Chimney Rock, and Sedona. Terraces in a trailside wash might trickle and splash with a seasonal stream in springtime. At 3 miles, an additional mile out to the playful Cow Pies, on a spur to the left, makes this an all-day (6-hour) adventure.

Drive from Uptown Sedona south on 179, cross the bridge just past Tlaquepaque, immediately go left onto Schnebly Hill Road, and follow the paved road until it ends with a parking lot on the left.

❼ DOE MOUNTAIN AND BEAR MOUNTAIN

One trailhead parking area serves two trails that climb in opposite directions. Doe Mountain Trail climbs 410 feet up a winding 1.25 miles to views in all directions from the flat mesa top. Bear Mountain Trail climbs 1,803 feet in 2.5 miles (5 hours roundtrip) to tremendous views of Fay

79

Canyon directly below, Dry Creek Basin, distant San Francisco Peaks, and an eastern horizon filled with red rock formations.

Drive to West Sedona, turn north at the stoplight onto Dry Creek Road, after 3 miles turn left at the Long Canyon Road intersection onto FR 152C, after 1.5 miles turn left at Boynton Canyon Road intersection, continue on the newly paved road 1.2 miles, and park on the left.

Loop *Hikes*

⓲ BELL ROCK/COURTHOUSE

Circling two landmark rock formations, this moderate 4-mile loop takes about two hours. Views include Cathedral Rock in the distance, Twin Buttes hiding the Chapel of the Holy Cross, Gibraltar, and the cliffs of Munds and Lee mountains.

Drive along 179 to the north end of the Village of Oak Creek, turn east into the Bell Rock Pathway Vista parking lot. Follow the trail sign to the Bell Rock Pathway which skirts Bell Rock until the loop trail is marked with 2-foot tall rock cairns.

❸ SECRET CANYON TO BEAR SIGN CANYON

This strenuous 7-mile loop (4 hours) begins on the Secret Canyon Trail surrounded by red rock cliffs, then at 2 miles branches to the right onto the connector David Miller Trail. This memorial trail ascends 800 feet in less than a mile in a charming forest before reaching white cliffs with desert plants and outstanding views. It then steeply descends into the dark, deeply forested Bear Sign Canyon for 3 miles to a parking area. Follow the dead-ended FR 152 (Vultee Arch Road) one mile back to the Secret Canyon Trailhead.

Turn right (north) at the stoplight in West Sedona onto Dry Creek Road; after 2 miles turn right onto FR 152, and after 3.5 miles parking is on the left.

Homes of the Ancients

❹ PALATKI IN RED CANYON

Archeologists named this 800-year old pueblo "Red House" in the language of the Hopi, descendents of the ancient Sinagua people who lived here. A guide takes you on a one-third-mile trail, explaining a series of pictographs made by several cultures and dating back thousands of years. A loop just more than one-half mile climbs the opposite direction to the picturesque, two-story stone dwelling hosted by volunteers.

Drive to West Sedona, turn north at the stoplight onto Dry Creek Road, after 3 miles turn left at the Long Canyon Road intersection onto paved FR 152C, after 1.5 miles turn left at Boynton Canyon Road intersection, continue 4 miles on FR 152C, which becomes a rough, dirt road, turn right at the FR 525 intersection, stay right at the next fork, and go 1.8 miles to the parking area. Red Rock Pass is required; reservation recommended; call 928-282-3854.

⓴ HONANKI BELOW LOY BUTTE

At the end of a remote dirt road, the largest ancient pueblo in the Sedona region sits inside an alcove on a terrace above a viewing area. Visitors are not allowed inside the multi-roomed structure.

Drive to West Sedona, turn north at the stoplight onto Dry Creek Road, after 3 miles turn left at the Long Canyon Road intersection onto paved FR 152C, after 1.5 miles turn left at Boynton Canyon Road intersection, continue 4 miles on FR 152C, which becomes a rough, dirt road, turn right at the FR 525 intersection, stay left at the next fork, staying on FR 525, and go 4.5 miles to the parking area on the left.

Hikers enter a piñon and cypress forest along Brins Mesa Trail. See Brins Mesa on Page 78 under "Vista Hikes."

Index